Looking Back...

A Dallasite's Recollections from the Roaring Twenties
to the New Millennium

by William E. Mott Jr.

Looking Back...
A Dallasite's Recollections from the Roaring Twenties to the New Millennium

ISBN-10: 0-9789601-0-6
ISBN-13: 978-0-9789601-0-0

Library of Congress Control Number
2006936933

Printed in the United States of America
1 3 5 7 9 10 8 6 4 2

Printed and produced by Lone Star Productions
For information, contact Ginnie Siena Bivona at 972-671-0002
ginniebivona@sbcglobal.net

Dedication

This book is dedicated to my loving wife, Barbara, without whom it would have never been written. She has stood by me and supported me loyally and faithfully since we first met back in 1941, as my only true love, helpmate, and confidant.

Contents

Introduction

While this is a compilation of the many memories in my mental storehouse, they would have been lost without the invaluable assistance contributed by my wife, Barbara, who did the original typing, and my son, Bill III, who edited and filled in a few memories and helped with the final draft. Even my grandson, Bill IV, added value by giving it a final check for any grammatical errors. It has been an endeavor of rich satisfaction, and one I hope will be enjoyed by all who read it.

I have lived in Dallas since my birth in 1922 and am a second generation Dallasite. There have been many books written about the early days in Dallas and some of the facts you find in this one may be familiar to you. I have been asked many times while speaking at Rotary Club meetings and other gatherings to share the wealth of information in my photographic memory by writing a book. So I did! I hope you find these pearls of information as interesting as I did when I experienced them.

I wrote this for two reasons: For the many recollections I have of a city in growth from the 1920s and some of the interesting aspects of this growth as witnessed by my family, friends, and me, and to inform my children and grandchildren of a time long past, and of some of the ancestors who played a part in the history of the Mott and Abbott families. It is both autobiographical and historical. Let's do a little strolling down memory lane together.

Chapter One

THE FAMILY

My family is very proud of its four generations, all having been born and raised in Dallas. My father, myself, my son, and my grandson have each carried the same family name, William Etheridge Mott. I always said if I became distinguished enough I would change my name to W. Etheridge Mott, but I'm running out of time.

This became a little confusing in later years, as my mother called all of us "Billy," and we had to figure out just who she was referring to. At Christmas, when the family was all gathered around the tree and "Santa Claus" was passing out the presents, one after the other he called out "To Billy from Mama." We never did break her of the habit, but we did finally learn which Billy got the gift and which mother was Mama.

Dallas has been very good to me, and I have always said if you can't make it in Dallas you had better hang up your suit. It has been through hard work and diligence, but I have enjoyed the better things that reward those who strive to obtain a good and peaceful life.

My wife, Barbara, and I have benefited from a rewarding blissful union since 1945 and have been blessed with two happy and productive children, Bill III and Cathy, and two wonderful grandchildren, Bill IV and Jordan.

When they wanted to know, I have been able to tell them about how things used to be and how one's early life forms the basis for what kind of person one becomes. Today's world is nothing like it was a generation or two ago, and I feel that knowing something about what came before can be very helpful in understanding the present world that we know today.

However, this world is changing so fast these days it will keep the historians pretty busy keeping up with all of the mind boggling new things we would never have dreamed of in our wildest imaginations during the time I was growing up.

Being part of the older generation, I find myself longing sometimes for the less stressful, more peaceful existence we knew back then, even though things were physically more difficult and there were fewer challenges to "keep up with the Joneses." On the other hand, it is hard to complain about the labor saving devices we all enjoy, and, as a result, I have no desire to go back to "the good old days."

Take computers, for instance. My wife had the tedious job of putting all of this down as I talked, and she had to take a computer course to learn how to "word process," but in the long run it wouldn't have happened without that little modern marvel — the computer. She started to do it on her electronic typewriter (an improvement in itself over the old machines) but it didn't take long to decide that this book wasn't going to happen if we didn't step up to the new technology.

For those of you interested in genealogy, this chapter addresses how the Mott family came on the scene in Dallas.

My father, William E. Mott Sr., was born on November 3, 1896 in a house on the corner of San Jacinto and Germania, which was renamed Liberty Street during World War I, and was thought to be more desirable than any name that smacked of Germany during the war years. His mother and father had been married in Cochran's Chapel on the corner of Northwest Highway and Midway Road a few years previous to his birth. The church is still active and is located on its original site.

His mother, Mary Eliza Hill, along with her family, had moved to Texas shortly after the Civil War, primarily for her father's (William Pembroke Hill) health. They settled first in Pilot Point, Texas where Great-grandpa Hill, in partnership with another man, purchased a general mercantile store with the money he had received for his farm in Alabama.

I have been told that the partner was a bit dishonest and wound up with all of Great-grandfather's money. Mr. Hill was said to be a gentle, trusting man and had served in the Confederacy. He was an aide to General Forrest, and I am told that his name appears on Stone Mountain in Georgia. After being captured by the Union Army, he was freed to go home and work the farm because of his very young age, providing he would pledge to never again bear arms against the Union.

My grandmother, his daughter, used to tell that she and her family, consisting of her sister, Claudia, and brothers Robert, Thomas, Rutherford Etheridge, and Great-grandpa Hill, moved to Dallas and embarked on what my grandmother called the produce business. I think in reality it was only a horse-drawn vegetable wagon. Being a rather proud woman, she was inclined to embellish the facts a little, but it did elevate the status of the endeavor somewhat.

Had he been a garbage man, she probably would have referred to his occupation as a sanitary engineer.

In his later years, Great-grandpa Hill used to enjoy spending his afternoons at the Happy Hour Theater, which was located on Akard Street between Elm and Pacific. This was a well-known burlesque house, where he enjoyed watching the girls and was a regular patron. With his flowing white beard he was quite a distinguished looking gentleman.

One day when crossing Elm Street a young lady spoke to him in a familiar way and he replied that he didn't think he had made her acquaintance. She responded with a smile and said that she recognized him from the front row at the Happy Hour. I don't know if he was pleased with the recognition or embarrassed, but I rather imagine he was flattered to have been noticed by such a lovely young lady.

His attraction to the ladies was not limited to the girlies on the stage, for when my mother and father were first married he asked my mother to lift her skirt just above her knees so that he might admire her legs, which were nicely shaped. She was greatly offended by his request, and always considered him to be a dirty old man.

When his grandson Harry was old enough to drive, he would chauffeur his grandfather on Sunday drives around town in his mother's Studebaker. If someone was poking along in front of them, Mr. Hill would get impatient and want Harry to honk at them to move over. He would tell Harry to "Make a fuss, Harry! Make a fuss!"

He must have been quite a character and a man of few words. On one occasion, when Lake Worth had just been completed in Fort Worth, a Sunday drive to view the new lake was planned. The whole family was included on such excursions and as they crested a slight hill, the lake came into view, at which time Great-grandpa Hill proclaimed, "There's the lake, let's go home."

I have been accused frequently of being brief and to the point myself, and I wonder if I maybe didn't inherit that gene. "Just quit the small talk and cut to the chase," I say. But sometimes we remember those little terse phrases people utter, like when someone asked Mr. Hill if he would like more iced tea he would say, "I believe so. Just cover the ice." That's a favorite of mine that has been passed down in time.

And to continue with the family tree part of this historic story (for my kids' information), my grandmother Mary Eliza Hill met William Henry Mott in Dallas where he had settled. William Henry was born November 15, 1865 in London, England. He had immigrated to the United States as a young man, settling first in Des Moines, Iowa, and later worked in the timber business in the Minnesota woods.

Their marriage produced three children, William Etheridge, Viola, and Harry Hill. William's middle name was taken from his uncle Rutherford Etheridge, known as R.E., and Harry's middle name was his mother's maiden name, Hill. Like the name William, I got tagged with the same middle name, Etheridge. It must be an English thing.

William Henry Mott was a very accomplished woodworker and worked in a mill located at Orange (now Field) and McKinney Streets on the site where the Bank of America's drive-thru now stands. He operated a shaper and did a lot of the fancy scrollwork inside the old St. Paul Hospital, which was located on Bryan Street very close to their home, and where the Bryan Place Addition now exists.

He also did much of the work in the Catholic Church located at Ross and Pearl Streets that is currently known as Our Lady of Guadalupe, but was formerly Sacred Heart Cathedral, with a Bishop in residence. Bishop Lynch was the residing Bishop for many years.

There is a very prestigious high school in East Dallas that bears his name. My granddaughter, Jordan, graduated from there.

William Henry, being an Englishman, was a lifelong Episcopalian and was regularly in attendance at All Saints Episcopal Church located at the corner of Ross and Peak. In later years this structure was moved to 3617 Abrams Road where it is in service to this day. He died on March 22, 1916 following complications from gallbladder surgery.

Mary Eliza was born December 25, 1874 and lived to be 97 years old, passing away on September 14, 1971. As a young woman in Dallas she contracted smallpox, which was epidemic at that time. It was the custom for the local health department to put quarantine signs on houses where there was a communicable disease.

This practice continued into the 1930s, which I recall vividly. Mary Mott's case was sufficiently serious that she was sent to a county facility then known as the Pest House, located where the present Parkland Hospital now sits. This is the same hospital where President Kennedy was taken after being shot in 1963. She asked one of the orderlies if she could take her meals somewhere that she did not have to look at some of the patients whose faces were terribly marred with sores from the disease. They gladly obliged her by erecting a screen behind which she could eat in private.

When she was released she went to the front desk and asked for the bill for the services rendered. Much to her embarrassment she was told that the Pest House was a county facility and that there was no charge. Fortunately she had no scars. After Barbara and I were married I found out that her mother had also had smallpox during that epidemic and had been a patient at the Pest House too.

Mary Mott was a very progressive lady for her day. After she was widowed in 1916, she embarked on a career selling life insurance to support her family. She was very successful and at one time won a trip to Port Huron, Michigan to the home office of the company for whom she wrote policies. This was a trip for two and being a widow, she took her youngest child, Harry, with her.

Even to the end of her life she remained sharp and interested in everything that was going on. She owned and drove a Studebaker at a time when very few women even drove. She loved to tell the

Mary Mott – age 25

story about driving her father in the Studebaker on a dirt road, and when the sand was quite deep she would downshift to second gear to maintain her momentum. At one point her father said, "Mary, you could do a whole lot better with this car if you would leave that stick alone."

Toward the end of her life she had to live in a nursing home in California, and she made the best of it, but she never got used to living around all of those "old people." She had a very keen sense of humor and an infectious laugh and never complained about anything. She could always see the good side of people regardless of their faults. No matter how bad they were or what terrible things they did, she always said she felt sure they had a good reason for their behavior.

She even smoked cigarettes in the privacy of the bathroom for many years but never inhaled. (Where have you heard that before?) Consequently it was very easy for her to give up smoking in later years. She wasn't a drinker, as such, but often enjoyed a small dram of whiskey, and she loved to play poker.

Unfortunately, all three of her children inherited or otherwise acquired an addiction to alcohol, which destroyed William's and Harry's marriages, and after Viola was widowed in her 40s she drank half a pint of vodka daily and suffered the physical consequences.

William E. Mott Sr., their first child and my father, first attended the Cumberland Hill School, which was on the corner of Akard and Munger. This was the nearest grade school to their home and was close to where his father worked. The building was completely restored into offices by former governor Bill Clements for his oil drilling business in the 1960s.

My mother's experiences in Dallas do not go back as far as my father's, since she and her sister Dorothy moved to Dallas in 1917 when her widowed father, Sidney G. Abbott, came to the city to become the assistant manager of the Oriental Hotel. They moved here from Hillsboro, Texas, where he managed the Wear Hotel.

My grandfather Abbott was born in Caledonia, Minnesota, where his father was a wagon builder. The name was originally Abbotts, but Sidney elected to drop the "s".

Many of the Abbotts lived in Caledonia for years, but Sidney moved to Chicago as a very young man where he was employed as a bellhop at the old Metropol Hotel. There he met a charming young chambermaid named Mary Catherine Lechnir, who had come to Chicago from her home in Prairie du Chien, Wisconsin and was staying with an older sister, Otillia Lechnir Olsen.

A romance ensued, and they were later married. This union was blessed with two daughters, Sydney and Dorothy.

Sisters – Sydney and Dorothy Abbott

In 1904 the city of St. Louis staged the Louisiana Purchase Exposition, and the railroads were doing a big business transporting people to and from the fair. It was about this time or slightly prior to it that Sidney Abbott obtained a job as a dining car steward where he was to begin his education in the fine food business. It equipped him well for a lifetime of hotel and club management.

Anyone old enough to recall being served in the dining car during the heydays of the railroads will never forget the high quality

Sidney G. Abbott

of the food and the unforgettable taste and aroma of the coffee they served in little silver pots. The waiters all wore white jackets and black trousers and bow ties.

The St. Louis Exposition was the first to be lighted electrically with alternating current. It was at this fair that the American public was first introduced to the hamburger, as well as ice cream cones.

All the railroads of the day ran special excursion trains to the fair, and Sidney was on the run from Chicago to St. Louis and back. A man approached him with the proposition that if he would allow him to ride from Chicago to St. Louis without a ticket, he would give him the lion's head ring he was wearing to hold as collateral until he was ready to return to Chicago, at which time he would pay for both tickets and reclaim the ring.

While these lion's head rings were very popular around the turn of the century, the design was also made up as cuff links and tie pins.

In those days, train crews were allowed to place items in the baggage car free of charge. This was known as "blind baggage," and Sidney made arrangements with the baggage master to allow this passenger to ride "blind baggage." The end result was that the man never returned to collect his ring, and Sidney began wearing it on a daily basis as his own.

When I was about five years old, we lived briefly with my grandfather, and I used to watch him shave each morning with his straight razor. He would remove his lion's head ring and place it on the side of the basin. I was just tall enough to look the lion in the eye as he stared back at me through his diamond eyes, with a larger stone in his mouth. I admired it so much that my grandfather promised to give it to me when I became 21.

On December 8, 1943, my 21st birthday, I received the promised prize ring. At that time it was my proudest, and almost only possession. I wore it constantly until July 7, 1973 when my son, Bill III, turned 21. The ring was handed down to him to continue the family tradition of inheritance on 21st birthdays. My son handed it to my grandson, Bill IV, on December 14, 2001 adding a third-generation Mott to the list of recipients, and Bill IV has said that once he is married, if he is blessed with a son, he will be naming him Bill Mott V, and will continue the tradition.

Lion's head ring

Following Sidney's days in dining car service he embarked on a change of career when he became involved in the hotel business as catering manager of the Peabody Hotel in Memphis, Tennessee.

After the early death of his wife, Mary, Sidney sent his two daughters to live with their maternal grandmother in Prairie du Chien, Wisconsin. He subsequently accepted the management position of the Wear Hotel in Hillsboro, Texas.

He left the Wear Hotel to come to Dallas to be the assistant manager and catering manager of the Oriental Hotel, which stood at the corner of Akard and Commerce Streets, catty-cornered from the Adolphus Hotel. This hotel was owned and managed by Otto Herold, who was also president of the State Fair of Texas and who owned the Oriental Laundry located on Young Street.

I'm sure they did the hotel laundry, which would have been a big account. It was at the Oriental Hotel that Sidney first met the chef, Marcel St. Crieq, a very skilled French chef who had previously been a chef on the Cunard Steamship Lines. This was to prove to be a long-time association and friendship.

During his tenure at the Oriental, Sidney found himself in a position to again provide for his two daughters, and brought them to Dallas to live with him. Dorothy, the younger, completed her high school education at the old Dallas High School, later to be known as Crozier Technical High School, on Bryan Street. After high school she returned to Prairie du Chien and enrolled in nurses training. Upon completion of her studies she returned to Dallas.

Her sister, Sydney, my mother, remained in Dallas and was first employed by a Greek candy maker and worked in his candy kitchen on McKinney Street near the present site of the Crescent Hotel. Since she was allowed to eat all the candy she wanted, it was hard on her figure, but she managed to keep her weight fairly normal in spite of the calories. Her second job was a stock girl and later a bookkeeper at the original Neiman Marcus department store, where she worked until she married.

My grandfather stayed with the Oriental Hotel until it was razed to make room for the new Baker Hotel, which was constructed on that site. His career then took him to Shreveport, Louisiana and he became manager of the Youree Hotel. He took the entire kitchen staff with him to Shreveport. Later he and Marcel came back to Dallas as manager and chef of the newly formed Dallas Athletic Club, which was located in a new building at the corner of Elm and St. Paul Streets.

He was hired away from the Dallas Athletic Club to manage the newly constructed University Club atop the Santa Fe Building on Jackson Street. This club was only accessible through the main entrance of the Santa Fe Building, where you took the elevator to the 10th floor and crossed an open sky bridge to the club, which was located on the 10th floor of the No. 2 Unit of the building.

Sidney was the secretary and general manager of the club and had the responsibility of purchasing all the furnishings, as well as employing the original staff. This was a very posh club and probably the only downtown club in Dallas at that time.

It opened February 24, 1927 and became "THE" place to go for the "Who's Who of Dallas." The architecture was of Tudor style, with the main ballroom having a huge open fireplace and the dance floor, when not in use, was partially covered with three enormous white Polar bear rugs with heads attached.

These made a big impression on a very small boy when I visited the club with my mother for lunch. On one occasion Richard E. Byrd, then Navy Commander and later Admiral, was feted with a luncheon at the University Club. He autographed a business card for my grandfather, and I have it in my collection of mementos.

Some of the major dignitaries of the day were members: E.B. Doran; John W. Carpenter of Texas Electric Services and Southland Life; Phil T. Prather, one of the developers of Highland Park; E.M. and G.B. Dealy of the *Dallas Morning News* and the *Dallas Journal*; Julius Schepps; E. Gordon Perry, the Dodge and Chrysler dealer; Otto Herold, president of the State Fair of Texas; I.J. O'Donald, a representative for Karl Hoblitzelle, Interstate Theaters; and many other prominent citizens.

Sidney left the University Club in 1928 to accept management of the new Hilton Hotel in Waco. Immediately following the closing of the University Club, the premises served as studios for WFAA Radio, from which the early morning show known as "The Earlybirds" aired daily for many years. Later, during World War II, the site was occupied and operated as the Chez Maurice, an upscale nightclub.

Sidney G. Abbott

My mother and father met while they were both working at Neiman Marcus. Earlier he had worked for Sanger Bros. department store prior to World War I. El Centro College now occupies this location.

He was inducted into the army on June 27, 1918 and assigned to the Provost Guard and stationed at Camp McArthur at Waco, Texas, where he received his basic training as an M.P. During his enlistment at Waco, a German submarine put off one or more spies on the Texas coast and one of them made his way north to Waco, where he was captured while climbing down off of their water tower.

He had poisoned the water supply. He was sent to Alcatraz Island in San Francisco, California, which at that time was a Federal army prison and was in the process of being hewn out of the rock.

The army dispatched my father to Alcatraz to pick up the prisoner and transfer him via train to the primary military prison at Ft. Leavenworth, Kansas. On his return trip he had to be taken from the train in San Antonio, Texas as he was suffering from a very severe case of influenza. It was in epidemic proportion throughout the United States and the armed forces, and millions of people were afflicted with it throughout the world. He was so terribly ill that he was placed in the terminal ward and was not expected to live. While he did recover, his lungs were badly scarred, and during subsequent hospital stays he would be diagnosed as tubercular until sufficient tests proved to the contrary.

After recovering from the flu, he returned to his unit, which was preparing for shipment to France. They were performing a military review and he was a passenger in a big four-wheel drive truck known as a Quad-Nash. As they approached the reviewing stand the driver stalled the engine, which had to be hand cranked.

Private Mott jumped out of the truck and engaged the crank to restart the engine. When the engine fired the driver was so flustered that he engaged the clutch and the truck lurched forward. Private Mott turned and attempted to run, but the truck knocked him down and in the process the crank handle hit him in the back. This required a stay in the hospital as his spine was severely injured. It also precluded his accompanying his regiment overseas, and resulted in a lifetime of back trouble, which made him somewhat hunchbacked.

Upon returning to Dallas he went back to Sanger Bros. and was re-hired despite the fact they thought he had died from his illness.

After he and my mother were married, he went to work for the Ideal Laundry Company as a route salesman, driving a Model T Ford truck.

William E. Mott Sr.   *Sydney T. Abbott*

Chapter Two

DOWNTOWN DALLAS - THE EARLY YEARS

My father remembered the Trinity River flood of 1908. He was approximately 12 years old and he and his father walked down the railroad tracks to the railroad bridge over the Trinity River. Being just a normal kid he wanted to venture out onto the bridge itself, but he was refused permission, and a little later, the bridge was washed out by the surging waters. The water rose into downtown Dallas and all the buildings in the area of the courthouse were flooded.

Following the flood of 1908 was the beginning of the drought of 1909 to 1912. During this time water was supplied by the Turtle Creek Reservoir, with the pumping station located at what is now Harry Hines and Oak Lawn, where it currently serves as an art center. The drought was so severe that there was not enough water to fill the water mains, and horse-drawn tank trucks delivered water to residents who provided their own containers.

Early on there were many laundries in Dallas, some of which were Ideal Laundry on Ross Avenue, Leachman's Laundry on Ervay and Hickory Streets, the Oriental Laundry on Young Street, and Yate's Laundry on College (now Hall) and Florence. There was a huge laundry called the Oak Cliff Laundry located just at the west end of the Houston Street viaduct, which was the only viaduct across the Trinity River. Their billboard showed a picture of a big woman, and their slogan was "Oak Cliff's Largest Washerwoman."

Washing machines in the home were indeed a rarity and the laundry route man would pick up your dirty clothes at your home and return them all starched and ironed. This was a very big industry in Dallas and other cities as well.

At home, laundering was done by using a washboard in the bathtub or in a wash pail and was a very labor-intensive operation. One of the happiest days of my mother's life was when she was able to buy a washing machine with an inheritance from her grandmother.

There were no steam irons, either, and most clothing was made from pure cotton fabrics, which wrinkled terribly when washed. The wash water had "bluing" added to make the white things whiter, and a starch solution was made by adding water to starch powder and boiling it a few minutes. It was then cooled down with more water and the clothes that were to be stiffened were then doused in it before being hung out to dry. They were then hand "sprinkled" and rolled up tightly to distribute the dampness, and sometimes placed in the icebox for a while.

One innovative device developed for this purpose was a bottle stopper with a few holes punched in it and inserted into a soft drink bottle full of water.

Most of the clothes dryers were of the solar kind: Two metal poles with T bars at the top set in concrete about 20 feet apart with four galvanized wires stretched between them. The sun and wind bleached and dried the clothes and they smelled so fresh and nice.

One of the best memories of that era was the pleasant experience of climbing into a bed with fresh sheets and pillowcases straight from the clothesline.

Some families were able to afford a black woman who came to the house once a week to do the wash. She built a fire in the backyard and placed an iron wash pot over the embers to get the water hot. She used a washboard to scrub the clothes clean.

1922 was a momentous year for Dallas as it marked the construction of the Magnolia Building at the corner of Akard and Commerce. It was built by the Magnolia Petroleum Company, which today is known as the ExxonMobile Company. It was then the tallest building west of the Mississippi and remained Dallas' tallest building for some 20 years until the Mercantile Bank Building was constructed on the site of the old Central Post Office at Main and Ervay Streets, running through to Commerce.

The Magnolia Building had its own artesian well, and a cold drink of water from the water fountain was a refreshing treat on a hot summer's day. The building was not air-conditioned at that time, and all of the downtown office workers had to suffer the hot summer days with open windows and ceiling fans.

Harwood Street was "new car row" in the late '20s and early '30s. The Pierce-Arrow dealership had an inside ramp up to the second floor where the body shop was housed. This kept the noise away from the showroom and service department, which was on the first floor.

The building had a dumbwaiter about the size of a phone booth but only half as tall. Since my Uncle Harry worked for Pierce-Arrow, as a small boy of six or seven I was allowed to ride up and down with the parts sent up to the body shop. The dealership used a Pierce-Arrow wrecker, which I thought was the height of class.

In the late '50s and early '60s, we at the NAPA warehouse, located at 1719 N. Harwood St. rented the old Pierce dealership building for use as a piston ring, muffler, and tailpipe warehouse. A number of our employees watched from this building on that fateful day in November of 1963 as President John F. Kennedy and his entourage drove past on their way to the Apparel Mart on Stemmons.

Harry Mott and Dorothy Abbot were married in 1928, and lived in Dallas. Harry sold Pierce-Arrows during the heyday of the East Texas oil boom. All salesmen were required to buy their demonstrators on an installment contract. I suppose this was an effort to limit the dealer's liability.

Uncle Harry and Aunt Dorothy used to drive his demo down to Kilgore, Texas and check into the hotel where all the wildcatters stayed, since this was a prime location for an immediate sale to a wildcatter who had just brought in a new gusher, and who would otherwise have to drive to Dallas to purchase a symbol of his newfound wealth.

This practice was followed by many luxury car salesmen of that day. One morning Harry was awakened by a lot of commotion outside the hotel. This was before air-conditioning, and all of the windows were open for ventilation. Looking out the upper floor window, he spotted a car salesman who had just arrived in town with a new Duesenberg, and that created quite a stir since few people in East Texas had ever seen or even heard of a Duesenberg.

Duesenbergs were built in Indianapolis, Indiana, and were the costliest automobiles built in the United States at that time. Pierce-Arrows were a favorite car among the East Texas wildcatters.

1930 Model J Duesenberg

One day a man drove into the Harwood dealership and he and his car were completely covered with crude oil. It seems that he had just brought in a gusher that went over the derrick. He fired up his old Pierce and drove it through the torrent of oil and didn't stop until he drove into the dealership in Dallas where he promptly bought a new Pierce.

One of the oil men who drove Pierces was Mr. Hubbard, the father of Ray Hubbard Sr., for whom the local lake is named. They lived next door to my aunt and uncle on Bryan Parkway in what is now the Swiss Avenue Historical District.

Uncle Harry would take Mrs. Hubbard to the grocery store when Mr. Hubbard was in East Texas, since this was prior to the two-car family.

After Mr. Hubbard struck it very rich in oil they moved to a new house on Lakewood Blvd., but he continued to buy his Pierces from Harry as long as he sold them. The last one he had was a 1936 coupe. Today this car would enjoy the designation of a "Full Classic" as recognized by the Classic Car Club of America.

In the recent book *The Murchisons*, it tells how young Clint, John, and Burk were driven to Highland Park schools in a Pierce-Arrow. I don't know if Harry sold Clint his Pierces, but he might have.

One day the dealership received a call from a very irate lady in Highland Park who reported that a yardman who lived in the servant's quarters across the alley from her house had a Model A Ford to which Pierce-Arrow headlights had been skillfully installed on the front fenders, just like the headlights that the Pierce was known for. She had been told when she bought her Pierce that headlights on the fenders were a patented feature and she considered this a blatant infringement on the patent.

Of course it was not, since this was a case of customizing and not of manufacture for resale. But it sure did dress up that Model A.

Many bootleggers also liked Pierce-Arrows. One such person named Mickey Ray was a repeat customer of Uncle Harry's. Mickey had a young man who delivered bootleg corn whisky on an old motorcycle. Transportation came in whatever means to the end.

This delivery boy's name was Benny Binion, later to be recognized as the gambling czar in Dallas during the Roaring Twenties and the Thirties, and went on to Las Vegas to build and operate the famous Horseshoe Casino there.

My father knew Benny from the time they were young men, as

they were both avid dove hunters and hunted together occasionally.

One time Benny borrowed a double barrel 12-gauge Fox shotgun from my dad. An employee of Binion's who went by the nickname "Double" was indicted for killing a man and the borrowed gun was reported to be the death weapon.

The sheriff impounded the gun as evidence and my dad was forced to wait a long time before the trial was over and the gun was returned to him.

I still have the gun but I don't recall whether or not "Double" was convicted. In 1997 I had the gun enshrined in a frame and gave it to my son for his 45th birthday. He has it proudly displayed in his office.

The Pierce-Arrow agency later moved to a building that stood at the corner of Pacific and Preston Streets, which is now Central Expressway. It was during the 1932-34 operation of the Pacific Street agency that Pierce-Arrow had Ab Jenkins drive the 12-cylinder roadster to many 24-hour world records on the Utah salt flats. The film of this feat is still available.

As the depression deepened, the sale of luxury cars became so few and far between that my uncle had to give up this pursuit and go to work for B. F. Goodrich Rubber Company.

The dealership under Johnny Vilbig's ownership took on Auburn, Cord, and Duesenberg and moved into a smaller storefront building in the 2100 block of Main Street across from the old Central Fire Station. Johnny Vilbig also owned Star Foundation Company, which was located at Elm and Hall Streets, where a Bank of America Drive-thru is located today.

The two most prominent dairies in Dallas were the Metzger and Tennessee dairies. During the late '20s and early '30s all of the delivery vehicles were horse-drawn wagons with steel rimmed wheels. Metzger had one such wagon that had rubber tired automobile wheels and an auto radio that operated off of a storage battery that was recharged every night. This wagon was awarded to the top milkman for his use for one week, much like the employee of the week is recognized today with a special parking place.

The horses that pulled these wagons were very smart and knew the routes as well as the milkman. The milkmen carried metal baskets in which six quart glass bottles would fit. They would bring the milk into your home and put it in the icebox.

We took milk from Metzgers and our deliverer was named Mr. Baumgartner. He never could seem to understand that my mother was Mrs. Mott and insisted on calling her Mrs. Botts. So in return she started calling him Mr. Nussbaum and he would correct her immediately, at which time she would inform him that *her* name was Mrs. *Mott.*

On the way back to the dairy, which was out on South Lamar near the Trinity River, the drivers would water their horses at the granite water trough that sat in the middle of the intersection at Commerce and Preston Streets. This watering trough was also utilized by farmers who brought their produce to the farmer's market that was nearby on Pearl Street, between Jackson and Canton Streets.

The farmers would back their wagons up to the curbs and customers could walk up and down the sidewalk and buy right off the wagons while the horses stood for hours until it was time to return to the farm. The watering trough stood at this location for many years after horse-drawn vehicles were last seen on the city streets.

The fountain was restored many times by the city. It was so designed originally that as it filled and overflowed, the water ran into four catchments on each side of the base so that dogs also could drink from it. The waterspouts were in the form of lion's heads, which were bronze, one on each side of the fountain. It has been removed, and in recent years has been relocated in Old City Park, which is a very appropriate location for such a grand symbol of early Dallas.

I did see a fountain identical to it in the garden of one of the mansions in Newport, Rhode Island. It was identified as one that had stood in downtown Newport during the horse and buggy era, but had been rescued from obscurity by the historical society that had restored and maintained many of those magnificent mansions in that city.

During those horse-drawn days, ice was delivered by icemen,

who usually used a wagon pulled by a mule. Icemen wore heavy leather back protectors, which had a turned-up roll at the bottom for the purpose of catching the water from the melting ice they carried on their back and diverting it away on each side. This kept their trousers dry.

Ice was sold in blocks of 25, 50, 75, and 100 pounds. This was accomplished by pre-scoring the 100-pound blocks with a saw at the ice plant so that the iceman could take his pick and separate the desired amount from the larger block. Most houses had screened-in service porches where ice and milk could be delivered without the service man having to enter the house.

The gas and electric meters were located on the service porch so the meter readers could have easy access to them as well.

Some people ordered the same amount of ice every day, but those who had need for varying amounts in the event of company or a party used a four-sided card furnished by the ice company, which was placed in a front window, and had large numbers so printed that the one at the top indicated the amount of ice needed that day. Each time the card was turned it indicated a different amount.

We did not take ice from the iceman, but my father would pick up a 25-pound cake from the original Minyards grocery and icehouse on Lindsley Avenue. Each icehouse had three chutes with levers outside that when pulled delivered out the shoot a 25-, 50-, or 75-pound cake of ice. After making his selection, my dad would place the block of ice on one of the wing bumpers of his Model A Ford where the hot metal of the bumper melted its way into the ice and anchored it there for the short trip home.

Wing bumpers were short lengths of bumpers that were placed on each side of the spare tire at the rear of most cars of the day. The wing bumper disappeared with the advent of the spare tire being carried in the trunks of the cars. Rear mounted spare tires were not seen again until the introduction of the Lincoln Continentals in 1940.

As small boys my friends and I would run up to the back of the ice wagon while the iceman was in the house delivering the order and pick up the few chips of ice, or snow, which were always present where he had separated the small blocks from the 100-pound cakes, and we would eat it to cool off on a hot summer day.

When my mother and I visited in Wisconsin I introduced my cousin to this practice, but when the parents found out what we were doing they told us we should not eat any of the ice from the ice wagon since it was river ice from the Mississippi, which had been sawed the previous winter and stored in a well-insulated icehouse for later sale during the summer and was intended only for cooling and not for human consumption.

I have a feeling the reluctance to use ice in drinks in the upper half of the country came from this practice long after the advent of pure ice manufacturing came into practice in the north. We still refer to lightly iced tea as Yankee iced tea. Because of the hot climate, ice plants were numerous in Dallas. Two of the larger plants were owned by the Kennemer family and the Jodie Thompson family. The Thompson family was responsible for starting convenience stores at their ice dispensing locations throughout the city.

The first was a U-Totem store in Oak Cliff. This venture grew into what is today known as the 7-11 stores, and their skyscraper headquarters was originally built on Central Expressway near the location of their original ice plant.

Iceboxes began to become outmoded in the 1930s and electric refrigerators were much more desirable, even though they would be considered almost primitive when compared to today's models. Most were only five to six cubic feet in capacity, and only had space for two or three ice trays in the freezing compartment. There was no room for food in that area, and nothing could be frozen but water in the trays. The cubes stuck to the grids in the trays and it was necessary to run tap water over them to release the ice.

Electric refrigeration eliminated the need for a drain under the refrigerator as was necessary with an icebox. The water from the melting ice had to be disposed of. If you lived on the ground floor you could drill a hole in the floor and let it drain under the house.

All of this convenience was a boon to the housewife, but nevertheless it still had its drawbacks. If you lived on an upper floor, you had to put a pan under the icebox to catch the melting ice and it had to be emptied daily. If it happened to run over, it would damage the ceiling of the lower floor. As a result, people never were in danger wearing out their welcome, since they had to leave after a short time in order to return home and empty the icebox drain pan.

Electric refrigerators were a great improvement, but they weren't perfect due to the frost build-up in the freezer compartment that made it necessary to defrost the unit every couple of weeks. This was usually done by turning off the box, filling the ice cube trays with hot water, and waiting for the frost to melt into the glass tray beneath the freezing compartment.

Of course nowadays this is all done automatically with no muss or fuss. To me, having ice cubes dispensed through the door and ice cream always available are two of the best features of modern refrigeration. Early electric refrigerators were quite expensive and oftentimes cost as much as a new Ford, but they lasted a lot longer.

Some of the early General Electric refrigerators dating back to the late '20s and early '30s are still in operation and are considered prized possessions by nostalgia buffs and collectors.

During the depression, people's resourcefulness was unbounded. Men came to the door and asked if you had any old gold they could buy. They carried with them a small bottle of acid, and if someone had some gold frame eyeglasses or jewelry that had belonged to some deceased member of the family, or were ready to part with some of their own jewelry for ready cash, the bargaining would begin. After applying a drop of acid to the object to determine if it was in fact solid gold or merely gold plated, which determined the authenticity of the metal, a price would be agreed upon and the deal transacted.

Also, knife sharpeners went from door to door asking if any cutlery needed sharpening. They would perform the chore on the spot, collect their small fee, and go on to the next house. There were also clock and watch repairmen soliciting business door to door. An elderly man came to our door asking if we had any clocks to repair and my mother, having an antique china clock that had belonged to her grandmother, and needing repairs, told him she had a clock that needed fixing but that she didn't have any money.

He told her that if she had any canned goods he would repair the clock for some canned goods, which he did, and the clock is still operational today and belongs to our daughter, who prizes it as it had belonged to her great-great-grandmother.

Our neighbor Mrs. Roney was forced to set up a classroom in one of her bedrooms and teach preschool children and provide income, since her husband had been furloughed from T&P Railroad.

Not everybody had an automobile since public transportation was dependable and inexpensive. Many people who did own cars at the onset of the depression elected to store them in their garages because they could not afford to license and operate them.

A man working downtown could commute to work for seven cents each way by streetcar, or reduce that amount if he elected to buy tokens, which were six for a quarter. A number of men on our street worked for the railroads in clerical capacities and all were furloughed off from time to time since all the railroads were in hands of receivers who were attempting to get them back to solvency.

The Great Depression began with the stock market crash of Black Friday, October 24, 1929. On that day many people who had all their money and all they could borrow invested in the market were totally wiped out by the crash. Some jumped out of tall buildings or committed suicide by other means.

They were unable to face poverty, and some had insurance policies that they hoped would support their families after their death.

Dallas banks as well as banks nationwide began to fail.

At the onset of the depression, banks and lending institutions began to foreclose on their collateral consisting of homes, farms, automobiles, etc. As the economy worsened, they were unable to resell what they had repossessed. Consequently they were unable to pay the depositors the monies they had in the bank.

Many people in our neighborhood lost their automobiles to foreclosure. But after a while the lenders became more hesitant to repossess properties and began to negotiate with the borrowers to pay anything they could, and applied that to the interest that was accruing on the loan.

By 1931 there were eight million people out of work nationwide. The unemployment grew to 25% of the population. In every major city the dispossessed set up camps known as "Hoovervilles," making shelters out of old packing crates or anything else they could find. The Dallas Hooverville was located on Young Street on property adjacent to where the WFAA studios now stand. It was a concentration that covered several acres. The name "Hooverville" was a reflection on President Herbert Hoover, for whom many blamed the depression.

In the '30s and '40s Dallas was far different than it is today. Most all major shopping was done downtown. This was prior to the suburban malls that exist in most cities today. There were numerous first class department stores, such as Sanger Bros., A. Harris, Titche-Goettinger, Volk's, W.A. Green, LaMode, and of course Neiman Marcus.

In addition to these, there were several fine quality men's stores, including E. M. Kahn, Dreyfus & Sons, Jas. K Wilson, Gus Roos, Irby Mayes, Reynolds Penland, as well as other smaller shops that specialized in men's clothing. These stores were all accessible by streetcar from every corner of the city for only seven cents.

All of the department stores had elevator operators who called out each floor and the merchandise offered there. Titche-Goettinger had a large perfume fountain on the first floor in the cosmetic department that dispensed lovely perfume, and it was fun dipping your finger or handkerchief in the spray to sample the fragrance. Neiman Marcus' men's shop had an electric eye that operated the door. Kids would stick their hands in front of the beam to make the door open each time they went by.

Just down the street from Neiman's there was a downstairs bar known as the Pirate's Cave. They had embedded several silver dollars in the sidewalk in front, but they didn't remain there very long, as someone figured out how to chisel them out.

Under the intersection of Elm and Ervay Streets was a public restroom. In the men's side was a shoeshine stand with an attendant. I don't know what special feature the women's side had, as I was never in it.

There were three good dime stores: Woolsworth, S. H. Kress, and Grand Silver. They were great meeting places, as they all had bulk candy counters, and soda and lunch counters. There were numerous small cafes and restaurants to serve the office workers who were in town at noon.

Elm Street was known as theater row. There were approximately ten theaters in a three-block area. Their quality ranged from the palatial to the shabby. First was the Majestic (which survives today in a restored state), next was the Melba, the Tower, the Palace, the Rialto (which was a renovation of the Old Mill Theater), the Capitol (which played all western movies), the Mirror (later to be converted to the Telenews, which kept people up to date during the war in later years), the Queen, and the Fox (which was a burlesque house). The cost of movies at that time was 25 cents for matinees and 50 cents for evenings, and children's admission was a dime.

On stage at the Majestic regularly appeared vaudeville, big name bands, and even operettas. I attended a performance of *The Student Prince* at the Majestic, and when band leader Spike Jones and His City Slickers appeared, they broke all previous attendance records. The Majestic, Palace, and Melba Theaters each had pipe organs, which were originally installed to accompany silent movies, but they were occasionally played in later years.

All of the streets were filled with people day and night, and theater parking was provided by multi-story parking garages. In later years, when Barbara and I would drive down in our 1939 Buick convertible, the garage attendant usually parked it on the first floor, which was reserved for the most glamorous cars, making us feel very special.

Dallas always had the reputation of having well-dressed women, and no lady would even think of going downtown without her hat and gloves. There were men's hat stores as well as millinery shops for ladies.

The city was a great center for oil, insurance, banks, and real estate companies. The chief executives of these businesses were prominent civic leaders and very influential in city politics. It was alive and vibrant.

Chapter Three

MOM, DAD & ME IN THE ROARING '20s

When they were first married, my mother and father lived at 1721 Moser Street in the first block off of Ross Avenue. They lived there prior to and just after my birth. Mother became pregnant right away, and when the time came, the doctor was called and he actually came in his own car and took my parents to St. Paul's Hospital on Bryan Street where I was born at 7:00 A.M. on December 8, 1922. I was named William Etheridge Mott Jr. for my father.

As was customary, my mother remained in the hospital for two weeks after my birth. Imagine that! You can't stay that long today even if you have a double heart bypass.

In 1925 my parents moved to 1915 Summit, a street that parallels Greenville Ave. between Ross and Belmont. They rented one side of a duplex from Mrs. Petty, who lived on the other side. As was the frequent practice in those days there was only one bathroom, and it had to be shared by both tenants.

Some time after 1925, my father was employed by the Hoover Company selling Hoover vacuum cleaners door to door.

Early on, the Hoover Company sold directly to the public, and he and another salesman named Bob Willis worked together. They would work opposite sides of the street, knocking on doors and asking to be allowed to demonstrate the new Hoover vacuum cleaner. As was the custom, many people were still sweeping their area rugs with brooms or carrying them outside to be beaten on the clothesline.

There were special rug beaters that could be bought at any hardware store for that purpose. Part of the Hoover demonstration showed the housewife how the bag must be emptied, since disposable bags were far in the future.

It was a dirty, messy operation since the dirt went directly into a cloth bag and the contents had to be emptied onto a newspaper and disposed of in the trash. The sides of the bag had to be scrubbed together to keep the dirt inside loose so it would allow the air to pass through the bag.

When most of the streets in Dallas had been canvassed, the salesmen would get in their Model T Ford and call on homes in surrounding towns such as Garland, Wylie, Richardson, and Murphy. During one of their calls in Garland, the homeowner agreed to buy a Hoover if they would take his crockery butter churn in as a down payment.

This was agreeable, so Mott and Willis proceeded to take the churn out the front door and down the steps to the car. But in the process, Bob Willis started down the steps first with the churn, which had been placed on a small table to make it more portable, and my dad followed up the rear. As the table tipped downward the churn fell over and struck Bob on the head, knocking him out cold. After he came to he demanded to know "Who hit me?" The churn was loaded in the car and the table returned to the homeowner, but what happened to the churn after the mishap remains a mystery.

Bob Willis was a lifelong bachelor and lived with his mother until her death. She was a British subject and a very nice lady, and on one occasion she ordered from England a toy bakery truck filled with English tea cookies and gave it to me for my birthday.

Bob had a great sense of humor, and one day while demonstrating a Hoover he saw a man's picture on the wall of a prospect's home, and, in jest, he remarked to my dad, "Isn't that a great picture of Mr. McGivney?" He asked my dad to concur that it was a wonderful likeness of Mr. McGivney.

Whereupon the lady of the house insisted that this was not Mr. McGivney but a portrait of her father. Bob continued to press my dad to agree with him. My dad had a hard time keeping a straight face, as it was all a joke and there really wasn't a Mr. McGivney.

While living on Summit Avenue my mother hired a young black girl named Lula Mae to help look after me and another little boy named Charles Sears. This is an early example of babysitting, as Charles' mother worked outside the home.

I celebrated my third birthday while at this address and I received a little pedal car, which was the first of many cars to follow. I kept the sidewalk hot in my little car, followed closely by my buddy Jack, who was an excellent watchdog of questionable lineage.

My grandfather and his second wife, Rose, lived around the corner from us at 6531 Alta, and being so close I spent a lot of time there as she was so nice to me and I enjoyed my visits. One day my mother took offense at my attachment to Rose and suggested that maybe I would like to go there to live instead of with her. She began removing my clothes from the dresser drawer and I began to cry. I pled with her to stop, and her jealousy was allayed.

It was about this time in my life that my mother took me up to the Wise Barbershop where Charlie Wise gave me my first haircut.

Little did I know that 47 years later Charlie and I would be business associates in the Greenville Avenue State Bank.

My father was offered the opportunity to manage a new factory branch of the Hoover Company, which was to be established in Waco.

Our move to Waco was accomplished by calling the Central Transfer Company to move our furniture to 3105 Parrot Street.

My mother and I went down on the interurban, known as the Bluebonnet Special because it ran through numerous fields of bluebonnets between Dallas and Waco, while my father and our dog Jack followed in a 1926 Model T Ford.

The move went smoothly with one exception. Partway to Waco Jack decided that he didn't want to move, so he jumped out of the window of the Model T while underway and hit the ground running. It didn't appear to hurt him any since the car didn't run over 30 miles an hour, and my dad had to stop, turn around, and chase the fool dog until he finally caught him. From that point on he kept the passenger window rolled up.

My family needed some additional furniture since the duplex we moved from was very small. They went into downtown Waco to Stratton & Stricker Furniture Company where they bought a new bedroom suite, dining room suite, and two wicker rocking chairs.

The building that housed the furniture company was completely flattened in 1952 by a tornado that devastated much of downtown Waco.

Since my mother's father and her only sister lived in Dallas at that time as well as all of my father's family, which included his mother, brother, and sister, we came to Dallas very often on weekends in that Model T Ford and generally stayed with my Aunt Viola and her husband, Leo Dernier.

They lived in a large house on Bryan Parkway and my dad's brother Harry lived with them. We always celebrated Christmas with Aunt Vi and Uncle Leo since Christmas was a big thing with him.

I well remember the Christmas of 1926 when I got my tricycle. When we woke up Christmas morning everything was covered with snow and this was the last white Christmas we had in Dallas. We have come close several times since, but never quite has it happened.

The snow made it very hard for me to ride the new tricycle Santa had left the night before, but I put lots of miles on it after that. I also received my first bicycle, a 20-inch, on a subsequent Christmas on Bryan Parkway.

Between his business travels and all the trips we made to Dallas we wore out the engine in that Model T. At that time Henry Ford had an engine exchange program, which my dad took advantage of, and put a new engine in the car. Even at that early age I was interested in cars and insisted that he lift the hood and show me the new engine.

My mother was a practicing Catholic before she was married, and my father's family was Methodist. They were not married in the Catholic Church, but by Dr. Selectman, a Methodist bishop, and therefore she could not receive communion. Consequently they attended no church, but the people who lived across the street from us in Waco took me to Sunday school with them to the First Presbyterian Church in downtown Waco.

I was given a copy of the children's catechism, which my mother drilled me on until I knew it well. This prepared me for baptism, and when I was baptized, the minister was told that I had learned the catechism and he asked the other children who were being baptized if they didn't want to learn it too and they all said *no*.

Does this prove that if ignorance is bliss it is folly to be wise?

While we lived in Waco our dog Jack roamed the neighborhood. There was a man who raised rabbits at the other end of the block, and whether Jack killed any of them or not, I don't know, but the man suspected that he did, put poison out, and Jack ate it. He came home very sick and we called the vet and he came and picked him up in his personal car, but his attempts to save him were unsuccessful and there was great sorrow around our house because Jack was like one of the family.

We lived very near an army airfield, and when those early model bombers took off they flew very low over our house. It was great fun to wave at the pilots and see them wave back.

The Waco high school had a very good football team known as the Waco Tigers and their coach, Paul Tyson, gained an excellent reputation for coaching football and teaching the team members to be well-behaved gentlemen. They traveled to many out of town games, not only without unfavorable incident, but with praise from the public for their behavior.

Each year in the fall Waco had an exposition called the Cotton Palace, as Waco was the heart of cotton country.

One year the Hoover Company sent down a rather large balloon with "Hoover" printed on the sides. They also sent drums of helium so the balloon could be filled and flown over the Cotton Palace.

Unfortunately, the U.S. Army sent a group of soldiers to the Cotton Palace with the intention, no doubt, to inspire the young men there to enlist. Some of them arrived with live ammunition and they proceeded to shoot down the balloon, causing its untimely demise.

They were no doubt target practicing.

It was at the exposition that I first saw Paul Whiteman and his orchestra in the auditorium. A lot of the big bands would appear at fairs and expositions for short engagements. Whiteman had a world-renowned orchestra and it was they who first introduced George Gershwin's *Rhapsody In Blue* in the Aeolian Hall in New York City.

They had originally wanted to perform the piece at Carnegie Hall, but at that time it was considered too jazzy to be performed there. My, how times have changed.

Next to the Hoover display booth was a booth where men were handing out samples of a new product called *Feen-A-Mint*. It was a chewing gum laxative, and the men in the booth would ask some of the cotton farmers if they wanted some chewing gum. They gladly accepted the two-tablet sample and most popped it in their mouth and chewed it immediately.

No doubt some were unable or unwilling to read the instructions telling of its laxative properties. It didn't take very long before they returned to the booth, seeking directions to the nearest restroom.

Many expositions and state fairs of the day featured dirt racetracks, and auto races were held as one of the main attractions. In later years, I found out that Gene Fredrick, one of my friends and a noted race driver in the area, had raced regularly at the Cotton Palace. Race drivers in those days were very much like Gypsies, in that they trailered their cars from town to town following the various scheduled races, camping out wherever they could find a suitable place.

Even though we lived in Waco for about a year, our roots were firmly planted in Dallas and my mother and I would often ride the Bluebonnet Special from Waco to Dallas.

When the Hoover Company closed the Waco branch my dad accepted a job with an electrical supply company, which required us to move to San Antonio.

At first we lived in the Crockett Hotel, which is located directly behind the Alamo. The hotel has been completely restored and modernized in recent years and is still very much in operation. While San Antonio was our home base, we traveled with my father all over south Texas in a 1927 four-cylinder Chevrolet automobile.

In 1928 we moved back to Dallas and moved in with my grandfather right around the corner from where we formerly lived on Summit.

This was a very temporary arrangement while we looked for larger quarters. My Aunt Dorothy and Uncle Harry were also living there and it was very crowded.

For some reason, it was not at all unusual for several generations of families to live together. My mother grew up in her grandmother's house in Prairie du Chien, where her mother's brother and wife also lived.

When most houses only had one bathroom, I'm sure that caused a little problem, which was alleviated by the fact that they also had a deluxe two-holed outhouse in the back yard to expand their plumbing facilities, and was primarily used by the kids. Now everybody in the home seems to need a private bathroom.

A very important event occurred when my aunt and uncle purchased their first radio. I don't think there were but two stations on the air in the Dallas area. One was WRR, a municipally owned station, and the other was WFAA/WBAP. These two stations shared air time for many years.

In the afternoons, about 6:00 P.M., there was a broadcast on WFAA called "Sandman Soldiers." The two announcers were Jimmy Jefferies and Eddie Dunn. Jefferies was a well-known personality in Dallas for many years and I believe Eddie Dunn went to Chicago to work for one of the stations there.

Each evening the Sandman Soldiers would read off the names of children who had had birthdays that day, provided their parents had called in the necessary information. Needless to say, it was a great thrill to hear them announce on December 8, 1928 that Billy Mott was six, and my father and uncle both teased me by saying that the announcer had actually said Billy Mott was "sick" today.

Dallas was a much smaller city in the '20s as evidenced by the phone numbers we had. Our number was 8-5004 and we retained this number for many years, up until the '50s, even though we had lived in several different houses.

During our short stay on Alta Street I was privileged to see the giant zeppelin the *Los Angeles* come directly over Dallas. All predecessor zeppelins to the *Los Angeles*, being the *Shenandoah*, the *Akron*, and the *Macon*, were all destroyed in various storms. The *Los Angeles* had been part of Germany's reparation to the U.S. after World War I.

In the middle of December 1929 my mother and her sister Dorothy found a vacant duplex for rent at 6921-23 Lindsley Avenue in the Hollywood/Santa Monica addition, which was only partially built out. It was very convenient, with Will and Sydney and me occupying one side and Harry and Dorothy living in the other. The brothers Will and Harry had married the sisters Sydney and Dorothy, and this arrangement was very workable even with the usual shared bathroom. It was on the back side of the house and accessible from both apartments.

6921-23 Lindsley Avenue

In 1930 my cousin Harry was born, and he and I were double first cousins, as we both shared the same relatives with the exception of parents. Strangely enough, we were both only children, too, and felt almost like brothers.

Aunt Dorothy was a registered nurse but did not take any cases until after their son, Harry Hill Jr., was born. My mother was also a housewife but she would occasionally work during the Christmas season as an extra salesperson at Neiman Marcus at the only store they had at that time on the corner of Main and Ervay where she had worked prior to her marriage.

My dad was now employed by Oak Lawn Radio, which was an appliance store located at Oak Lawn and Rawlins.

Harry was still with the Pierce-Arrow dealership. The owner was Jack Reeves. Pierces were very fine cars built in Buffalo, New York and were driven primarily by the very "well-to-do." The dealership was on Harwood Street one block southeast of McKinney Avenue in a two-story building, one of three almost identical within a two-block area. One housed Pierce, one housed Studebaker, and one housed Franklin.

I recall Uncle Harry coming home one day and telling us that the Studebaker Company had purchased the Pierce-Arrow company and, much like today's leveraged buyouts and mergers, Harry was quite concerned about what the new ownership would mean to him and his future.

Jack Reeves subsequently sold the dealership to Johnny Vilbig. The Vilbig family, as I recall, consisted of three brothers, Johnny, E.A., and Lee. They were primarily in the excavating business and owned some vegetable truck farms out on what is now Irving Blvd.

There is a street known as Vilbig that runs off of Singleton Blvd., where once one of the best old car junkyards in Dallas existed, and auto restorers could buy parts for cars 50 years old.

In January of 1930 I was enrolled in kindergarten at Mount Auburn grade school on East Grand. It is still in operation today. Back in those days if your birthday occurred after September 1 you could not start school until the spring term in January.

Schools were overcrowded then much as they are today,

particularly in new areas of town where new homes were being constructed. I attended class in a two-room frame structure that sat on the east side of the main school building. They were called portables, since they were not intended as permanent facilities.

The rooms had wooden floors without any kind of floor covering and it took a lot of floor sweep to keep the dust down and the mud swept out that the children tracked in from the playground.

The heating was by an unvented gas space heater that sat in the room. It was very necessary for the teacher to keep the windows slightly ajar for fresh air to prevent asphyxiation. Air-conditioning was unheard of in schools or many other places.

Kindergartners were served a half pint of sweet milk in a glass bottle and two graham crackers as a mid-morning snack. When I was promoted to first grade we moved into the main building, where we had steam heat and a lunchroom.

All of the boys wore knickers and high socks, and during the winter months we wore lace-up high-top boots for warmth. The right boot always had a pocket high on the side intended for a pocketknife, so every boy had to have a pocketknife for his boot.

I always took my lunch in a workman type lunch box with a thermos bottle in it. They were painted black, as fancy colors and designs for lunch boxes were still in the future. My favorite lunch was a peanut butter and jelly sandwich. The lunchroom served a plate lunch with two vegetables and a meat for ten cents. Milk was three cents for a half pint. Our funds were too limited for me to buy my lunch, so I took mine every day.

The lunchroom had tables and benches and it doubled as an auditorium since it had a stage at one end. The tables could be stacked at the rear when necessary to make room for a performance.

On rainy days children were not allowed to go outside after lunch but had to stay in the lunchroom until the next class period started.

The school's furnace was oil-fired and a tank truck would come and fill the storage tank. Waste paper, which was considerable, was burned in an open incinerator out in the school yard that amounted to nothing more than an open top cage made of chain link fencing.

Bill Mott Jr. and his knife pocket boots and knickers – 1932

Wouldn't the EPA love that today! But this was the norm at all of the schools.

Each day after school an elderly man in a horse-drawn cart, which had been converted from a milk wagon, appeared across the street from the school. He sold soft drinks and candy bars and made hotdogs on a small stove he had in the cart. His name was Mr. Parker, and although only a few of the children had funds with which to make purchases, he was a friend to us all.

Early in my school years, while attending Mt. Auburn grade school, I rode my bicycle to school. But even in those long-ago times there were instances of vandalism to bicycles parked in the racks provided for that purpose. My bicycle was my prized possession and I never parked it at school, but was able to leave it on the front porch of one of my friend's homes nearby.

The bicycle I rode to school was nct my first bicycle. It was a new 28-inch that my dad had won in a sales contest, and while I had outgrown the 20-inch bike, the 28-inch was a very large bicycle for me when I received it.

I believe that big bike influenced my growth, as I had to stretch to reach the pedals. I took such good care of it that it was still like new when I gave it to my cousin Harry for use on his paper route in Athens, Texas many years later.

Bill and his 28" bike, with baby cousin Harry and a neighbor boy

Chapter Four

THE THREADBARE '30s

I have many happy memories associated with growing up in Dallas, but reality sometimes paints a painful picture. In those hardscrabble days there was no unemployment compensation, and the only assistance that people would accept was that which was extended to them by family, friends, or their church.

People were industrious and made a living with whatever talents they possessed. I vividly recall many of the ways they served us, and our neighbors. One elderly lady who lived many blocks away used to buy a large box of doughnuts and sell them door-to-door, one or two at a time. She said that she was an aunt of Tom Clark who served in the Roosevelt administration and was the father of Ramsey Clark, later to be Attorney General of the United States.

There were vegetable wagons, which were really mobile greengrocers. Some were horse drawn and some were motorized, but all of them utilized an old steel brake drum which they would strike with a metal object so that the housewives could hear them approaching and come out to the curb, usually in an apron, to make their purchases. This was a real boon, as they had no way to go to the store during the day.

In November 1932, Franklin D. Roosevelt defeated Herbert Hoover for the presidency of the United States. He did not take office until March 4, 1933 and began work immediately to stabilize the nation. As of March 6, 1933, the president declared a bank holiday and closed all of the banks that had not already failed.

They were not allowed to reopen until they had been examined and their position assessed. This created a great upheaval, but effectively stopped the runs on the banks that were epidemic with people trying to withdraw monies they had on deposit.

This really did not affect us, since we did not have any money in the bank anyway, but my great-grandmother in Wisconsin did lose money in the failure of the Prairie du Chien bank, particularly since she was a stockholder.

My mother and father, as well as my aunt and uncle here in Dallas, had no bank accounts, checking or savings, and did business on a cash basis. My mother would board the streetcar and go downtown where she would pay the light, water, and gas bills at teller windows in the City Hall, Lone Star Gas Company, and Dallas Power and Light Company, whose offices were all within a block or two of each other. Many people did this.

In about 1931, my Uncle Harry was finding it extremely difficult to sell Pierce-Arrows, and my dad was laid off from Oak Lawn Appliance at the same time. Since my dad had worked for the Hoover Company in earlier years, he told Harry that he thought they could make a living by servicing all makes of vacuum cleaners. He had gained experience in door-to-door selling while with the Hoover Company, so he and Harry would work the streets of East Dallas soliciting service and repair of vacuum cleaners.

Harry still had his old 1927 Pierce-Arrow, so they did have transportation with which to transport the vacuum cleaners they picked up for repair. They would knock on the door and ask the lady of the house if she had had her cleaner serviced within the last year as recommended by the manufacturer. Many homes had vacuum cleaners in dire need of repair. Some needed new electric cords, as well as new bags, belts, and lubrication. Most folks did not have the money to buy a new vacuum cleaner and hoped to get more service out of the one they presently had.

They would allow Will and Harry to pick up the cleaner, take it away for service in the old Pierce, which they had parked around the corner, and return it after they had fixed it. They had found a source for replacement parts for all makes of vacuum cleaners, which enabled them to repair any make or model.

They would come back home with the back seat of the car loaded with cleaners and then work late into the night making the necessary repairs so they could return the cleaners the next day, both looking and running like new. This provided both of our families with the necessary cash to pay the bills and buy groceries.

During 1933, Mr. Yonack, who owned the duplex at 6921-23 Lindsley, decided he wanted to remodel it and add a private bathroom to the small side and eliminate the shared bath feature that had existed since the house was built. He asked both my parents and my aunt and uncle to vacate so that he could do the remodeling.

I think we were slightly in arrears in the rent at that time, so we moved to 404 Clermont, a newer, very nice three-bedroom house. By this time my cousin Harry had been born, and he and his parents occupied one of the bedrooms, and my parents slept in one, and I slept in the third. It was a very congenial arrangement and we had no problem sharing the house since it was really an improvement over the Lindsley Avenue duplex.

The brothers Will and Harry continued to do vacuum cleaner repairs in the garage, where a workbench had been constructed.

When I first started selling magazines, my mother insisted that I save the first dollar that I earned. When I had enough change to do it, I purchased a silver dollar, which I planned to keep.

But we were so broke when we moved from Lindsley Ave. to Clermont that it had to be used to pay the moving man. In later years, someone accused me of having the first dollar I ever earned, and I replied that I did until I had to pay it to the moving man during the depression. He said he wished he could think of a reply that quickly, but little did he know that it was the truth.

One cold winter evening there was a knock on the door by a very nice looking young man who had come into Dallas on a freight train from which he had disembarked near Santa Fe and Clermont Streets. This was just a short distance from where we lived. He wanted to know if we would allow him to spend the night in our garage.

After holding a family conference, it was decided that it was too inclement outside, and Harry and Will took him in the Pierce-Arrow and drove him downtown to Deep Elm where they bought him a night's lodging in a walk-up hotel for 50 cents. By this time the repair business was modestly profitable, making life a little easier. People were quite compassionate toward those who were less fortunate, as they had all experienced leaner days.

One day Harry and my father encountered Mr. Yonack on the street in downtown Dallas. He told them that the remodeling of the Lindsley Ave. duplex had been completed for some time, but that he had been unable to rent either side. He invited us to move back if we could pay $25 a month per side. This called for another family conference, at which time it was decided that we could make do by renting only the larger side, where Dorothy and Harry could make an apartment on the second floor and we could use the bedrooms on the first floor. We would still share the bathroom, which now served only one side. We also had to share the kitchen, but since we had already been eating together this presented no problem.

The *Dallas Times Herald* newspaper ran a section of swap pages where people advertised for next to nothing anything they had to trade, and they would specify what they would like to trade it for. I'm sure this helped to increase the readership of the paper while it also proved to be a benefit to the people.

I never received any allowance. The Santa Monica housing addition was quite new when we moved to Lindsley Avenue and there were many unsold lots. But there was some new construction going on, and in order to capitalize on this activity I set up a soda water concession stand on the parkway in front of our house. My stock in trade was Coca-Cola and orange, creme, and strawberry soda. These I purchased from the Coca-Cola bottling plant, which was located on Second Avenue near Grand, just outside of Fair Park.

In those days the Coca-Cola company bottled all of these flavors. I sold the drinks for five cents a bottle, plus two cents for a deposit on the bottle if they wanted to take it with them. Business was quite good all that summer, and I operated it until the weather turned cool and I shut it down. Many youngsters from the neighborhood tried to entice me to sell to them on credit, but I steadfastly refused, since I had to pay cash when I bought them from the bottler.

It was always easy to tell when a new house was going to be built on a given lot, and I could see these workmen as new customers. The first indication was when a rickety old gravel truck would discharge about four cubic yards of gravel at the curb in front of the vacant lot. Within a day or two, a lumberyard would deliver the initial order of lumber, which consisted mostly of 2x4s and shiplap to be used in constructing the foundation forms. The workmen would begin arriving soon after the lumber and begin to dig pier holes, using a hand operated posthole digger. After the forms were completed and the steel installed, a cement mixer was brought to the site.

Mostly black men would start feeding the mixer with gravel and cement and water usually supplied by a neighbor's water hose. The cement mixer was powered by what was called a single cylinder hit and miss gasoline engine. It got that name because of the sound, which was very uneven in its sequence of firing.

After the foundation was poured and had set up, the forms were removed and used as siding on the exterior walls of the house. They were nailed on in a diagonal fashion in order to give the house strength and wind bracing. After the application of the shiplap, black tar paper was nailed to the exterior walls with common nails and little metal discs or washers.

When the structure was framed, a four-inch ledge was left on the foundation so the bricks could be laid just about like they are today. In reality, the homes in this part of the country are brick veneer, since the bricks play no role in the integrity of the structure. Brick homes in the North in the past had been constructed with solid masonry exterior walls. But due to the milder climate in Texas, brick veneer homes are inexpensive to maintain.

Before I graduated from grade school several of the boys in the neighborhood would ride to school with one of the fathers on their way to work. We would then walk home in the afternoons, and my favorite route was down the alleys between the school and my home. I picked up treasures that I considered to have some value.

One day on the way home I discovered that one of the city garbage trucks had burned out a transmission and the city had brought and installed another one and they had just discarded it in the alley. This was a find I could not resist, but I had to go home and get a small wagon to bring it home.

My mother would not allow me to bring any of my goodies on the property, so I had to stash them on the vacant lot next to our house. The lot became so littered that when the contractor decided to build a house he had to get a black man with a horse and wagon to gather up all the junk to clear the lot. I always did think that owning a junkyard would be a wonderful way to make a living. Just think of all the fabulous stuff you could buy and sell and play with.

During summer vacation from school, most of us played Monopoly by the day, all day long. It was kind of like a floating craps game in that the location changed almost daily, and we generally played on a covered front porch belonging to one of the players. No fair sitting on chairs and playing at a table. We all preferred to sit on the cool concrete with the board on the floor.

Many families whiled away the evening with card and board games, and bridge was an especially popular game among the adults.

Several of my grade school friends grew up to be quite well known personalities. Jack Evans, whose father ran a small storefront grocery store next to the East Grand Theater, followed in his father's footsteps in the grocery business with Wyatt's and Tom Thumb stores. He was later elected mayor of the city of Dallas.

Carroll Shelby also made an international name for himself as a race car driver and winner of the famed Le Mans 24-hour endurance race in France. This was the first race in which an American racing team was able to dethrone the very successful Ferrari team. Carroll went on to become a renowned performance automobile designer with the Shelby Cobra being his crowning achievement. Shelby won his first sports car race locally in a 1947 MG TC that I had formerly owned and sold to Ed Wilkins, another Woodrow Wilson school chum.

Another schoolmate, Dr. H. Neil McFarland, became a Methodist minister and missionary to Japan, and later professor of theology at Southern Methodist University.

Dan and Frank Kilgore were also schoolmates and lived out at the end of East Grand where it merges with Gaston Avenue and changes its name to Garland Road. Dan had been stricken with polio and wore steel braces on his legs and consequently was unable to walk to and from school. He and brother Frank would ride bareback to school on a horse that they would tie up to a tree on the east side of the school grounds where it adjoined Dr. Samuel's home place, which was later donated to the city and is now known as Samuels Park.

My father drove a company-owned 1930 Ford Model A Tudor furnished to him by Oak Lawn Radio where he was employed as a salesman.

On the other hand, my Uncle Harry had purchased a very nice used 1927 Pierce-Arrow. Occasionally (whenever invited) my mother and dad, Uncle Harry and Aunt Dorothy, and I would travel to Waco in the Pierce-Arrow, and for the weekend would live the good life at the Hilton Hotel where my grandfather was manager.

This is where I was introduced to filet mignon, shrimp cocktail, and other Chef Marcel St. Creiq specialties such as orange sherbet and consommé, all served in the room on fine china. At each place there was a serving of toasted almonds, and after the meal we were furnished finger bowls, which were fluted paper in silver bowls. My appreciation of nice things started early in life.

Our drive down to Waco and back was made at a consistent 50 miles an hour, which was a comfortable speed for the car and road conditions and was approximately 10 miles an hour faster than the majority of traffic that consisted of Model T Fords with a top speed of no more than 40 miles an hour.

Usually I was picked up before school was out on Friday for these weekend jaunts to Waco. One particular Friday while I was en-route to Waco, the plastered ceiling in the schoolroom where geography was taught came down in its entirety.

Fortunately they had some warning of the impending disaster and the children and teachers were outside during a fire drill and escaped the falling plaster. Globes of the world had just been installed on each desk in the room and they were all totally crushed to pieces.

We read about the happening in the Waco paper on Saturday before our return to Dallas.

In 1934 I made my spending money selling McFadden publications, publishers of *Liberty, Movie Mirror, Radio Mirror,* and *True Story* magazines.

True Story was a romance magazine published monthly, and was a favorite with elderly widows and spinsters.

Liberties were five cents and were published weekly. All the others were monthly issues and sold for a dime. I made one and a half cents per copy for *Liberty,* and three cents each on the others.

Other friends of mine sold these magazines, as well as *Saturday Evening Post,* which was a five-cent publication. I had customers who were unable to pay me weekly and I carried them several weeks until they could pay what they owed. I delivered these magazines all over East Dallas on my bicycle.

Mrs. Roney, who was a neighbor two doors down the street, baked nut bread in baking powder cans which her two sons, Billy and Jimmy, sold on their *Saturday Evening Post* routes. When I told my mother about this she agreed to make some of her very special orange marmalade and put it up in one-pint mayonnaise jars for me to sell to customers on my magazine route. This allowed me to make a little extra money over my magazine sales.

It was in 1935 that my father began to experience back problems as a result of his injury in World War I.

The Veterans Administration sent him to the Veterans Hospital in Muskogee, Oklahoma, which at that time was the nearest Veteran's Hospital to Dallas. He was given a thorough and complete examination, including psychiatric evaluation. He was discharged from the hospital and awarded a 75% service connected disability status, for which he received $75 a month.

This should have relieved our financial situation to some degree, but his addiction to liquor and gambling took precedence over household expenses and responsibilities. This made my mother rather hostile, but she had little influence over his wayward ways and rarely did she see any of the money.

He would meet the postman at the end of the streetcar line, which was a block and a half west of where we lived. There he would intercept the check, and he rarely made it home.

After my father started receiving his compensation check from the government and continued to be bothered by his back, he gave up the vacuum cleaner business, which was really more strenuous than he could cope with. The metal bodies of the cleaners were so much heavier than the plastic models we have today.

You could say that he went into retirement. This left his brother Harry needing an income. Somewhere Harry got the idea that a discount coupon book would be a saleable item if enough merchants could be persuaded to participate. We were still mired in the depression, and the concept of "buy one, get one free" was very appealing.

Harry did not have any capital with which to start this venture, so he approached Mr. Hubbard, the oilman who had lived next door to his sister and mother on Bryan Parkway, and convinced him to finance the venture. Mr. Hubbard always liked Harry and had appreciated his chauffeuring Mrs. Hubbard to the grocery store when he was out of town in East Texas buying oil leases.

Needing a place from which to do business and to store the inventory of Economy Books, Harry and Dorothy leased a small space of approximately 1,000 feet in a little storefront building on Lane Street just off of Commerce, near Neiman Marcus.

When they took possession of the space, they found that the Schrafft's Candy Company had formerly occupied it, and they had left behind boxes and boxes of demo candies. They were all real chocolates, but each piece was glued in place on the bottom of the box. Harry and Dorothy loaded them all up in the old Pierce-Arrow and brought them home to the duplex. We really didn't know exactly what to do with them, not knowing if they were edible or not, but a friend of my father's, a Mr. Gebhart from the old Oak Lawn Radio days, was over having dinner with us. He took one look, pulled out his pocketknife and cut a chocolate free of the backing and popped it in his mouth.

From that time on, it was free chocolates for all.

The Economy Book was produced by convincing a number of area merchants that the concept of "buy one, get one free" would lure repeat business to their respective establishments. Their businesses had been slow and they were willing to try anything to stimulate trade. The merchants included service stations, dry cleaners, independent grocery stores and drug stores, and other service oriented businesses.

Since Harry knew Earl Cabell, who was just getting his dairy and ice cream business established, he convinced him to do a "buy one, get one free" ice cream cone offer.

The first Cabell's dairy store was located in the Lakewood shopping center on Abrams Road. It had a large mockup of a double-dip ice cream cone affixed to the building, much like a barber pole.

As was the custom at some dairy stores, they gave curb service to their customers. One evening Harry and Dorothy, their son Harry Jr., and my mother and father and I pulled up in front and ordered six double-dip ice cream cones, which ordinarily sold for a nickel. When they were brought out to the car, we gave the carhop three Economy Book coupons and 15 cents.

She turned and rushed inside and showed the manager the Economy Book coupons. He hastily came out and confronted Harry, telling him he was not going to accept the coupons. He was a slender, middle-aged man and very agitated. Harry assured him that the coupons were valid and that he should call the main plant for verification.

This only added to his consternation, since the store only had a pay phone and he had to spend another nickel to call the plant. He did, however, and the plant confirmed the fact that he would have to accept the coupons. Due to inadequate advertising and marketing, the Economy Book was not a success, but it was very popular with us at the Cabell's ice cream store. Cabell's was more than just an ice cream parlor, it was also a dairy store, and they were famous for their fresh-churned buttermilk that came in a brown cone-shaped quart container that looked liked a butter churn.

Halloween in our neighborhood was a much-anticipated event. The mothers of my friends each had a specialty that they prepared each year.

Mrs. Roney always made popcorn balls, Mrs. Smith made some of the most delicious divinity you could imagine, and my mother made candied apples. All of these good treats did not prevent us from going door to door in the neighborhood where we were given apples, oranges, bananas, etc. We would generally wear costumes either homemade or improvised. Very few people had the means to buy a costume of any sort. Old sheets were very handy.

Our gang, consisting of Billy Roney, Al Smith, Walter Hunt, and myself, also did our share of mischief making. We would save old watermelon rinds and throw pieces up on people's roofs. They would come down bumpity-bump and startle the occupants of the houses.

We would also venture a block and a half up the street to the end of the streetcar line, where we would lay in wait in the bushes for the streetcar's arrival. Upon reaching the end of the line at Lindsley and Monte Vista, the motorman had to reverse the direction of the trolley in order to go in the opposite direction. He would then take his coin box, money changer, and control handle to what had been the rear of the car, where he would thus be ready to proceed in the opposite direction back to town.

As soon as the car started to move, one of us would run out and pull the trolley off of the overhead wires, at which time the car would go dark and the motorman would have to go to the rear of the car and put the trolley back on the line. Sometimes while he was doing this, one of the bad boys would push the bumper on the front of the car, which dropped the pedestrian catcher down on the track.

Some of the motormen were wise enough to leave both trolleys up for a short distance before lowering the front trolley. Several blocks toward town there was an uphill grade, and while we never greased the tracks, kids who lived closer to the hill did this with regularity.

You never know what goes on in your neighborhood to cause a little excitement. A young couple that lived in the house directly across the alley from ours used to walk around the block pushing the baby carriage with their baby in it, and they were always very friendly.

We were all surprised when the father was apprehended in the process of robbing a grocery store, for which he was convicted and sent to prison. While he was imprisoned, we often wondered about the man in the big Packard coupe who frequently called at their home. Little did we know that the man was the husband's lawyer, who was taking advantage of his absence to have a little hanky-panky with the lonely housewife.

Upon release from prison, the man came home and found the lawyer in his house. This would not qualify as the best form of legal defense, and the husband dismissed the lawyer's service with the help of a .38 revolver.

I understand that the couple just left the body lying in the hallway and called the police. I don't recall the outcome of the shooting, but I don't think he was convicted for it. I think this was a good example of what qualifies as "frontier justice." In later years this same woman was a known companion of Clyde Barrow's sister.

Another bit of neighborhood excitement occurred when in the middle of a summer night a bomb exploded in the front of a house on Monte Vista. It did extensive damage to the house but no one in the house was injured. The story goes that someone placed the bomb under the front bedroom window. It was told that he was a spurned suitor of a lady schoolteacher who lived at that address. Neighbors came from blocks away to witness the damage. It exploded with such force that some of the bricks were blown up into the trees where some of them lodged temporarily.

Ordinarily it was a pretty quiet neighborhood, but love does strange things to people.

Radio played an important part in families' lives, and all the youngsters in our neighborhood would listen during the summer to the soap operas of the day, some of which were "Ma Perkins," "One Man's Family," "Jack Armstrong the All American Boy," "Just Plain Bill," "Barber of Heartville," "Orphan Annie," "Stella Dallas," and "Vic & Sade," which was a particularly funny show depicting a couple who had a son named Rush. Vic worked for a company whose executives were Mr. Y.Y. Flurch, who Vic referred to as Mr. Y.Y., and Mr. B.Y. Flirgerian. There was a garbage man (now known as a refuse collector) by the name of Mr. Gumpock.

Mr. Gumpock was a very conscientious worker and stated that some of the younger fellows could possibly do a better job of handling the coffee grounds, but that he felt he was one of the best garbage men around. When Vic bought a new pair of shoes, he hated to have to break them in, so he let Mr. Gumpock wear them on his garbage route until they were broken in and he would then return them to Vic.

I don't recall who the writers were for this show, but they had some great material and later went on to write for TV. It could have been Goodman and Jane Ace, who were well-known comedy writers of the era, and had their own radio show called "Easy Aces."

In the evening after dinner, the adults especially enjoyed programs such as "Lux Radio Theater," "First Nighter," "I Love a Mystery," "Fibber Magee and Molly," "Jack Benny," and of course, without fail, "Amos 'n' Andy."

Everyone looked forward to the fireside chats by President Roosevelt. Sporting events were an important feature of early day radio, and boxing matches, football, and baseball games were broadcast on a regular basis. Most people had only one radio and it tended to be a unifying factor in that the whole family gathered around to listen.

During the late '30s the Dr Pepper Company sponsored a radio program that was originally broadcast from the roof garden known as The Peacock Terrace of the Baker Hotel. The shows were aired early Sunday evenings and were strictly a local production. The emcee and lead man was a gentleman named Roy Cowan, who was in the advertising business.

The show also featured a young lady who participated in comic skits with Roy Cowan. Her stage name was Ludie Mason, but my Aunt Dorothy said her real name was Ludie May Sensabaugh, and they had attended high school together at the old Dallas High School on Bryan Street, later known as Crozier Technical High School.

The sound man for the program was a Dr Pepper employee named Mr. Millican, but he was referred to on the show as Butch. He provided all the sound effects such as doors slamming, horse's hooves, wind storms, etc. All radio shows of the day had to have a sound man to make the action more realistic, and it was interesting to see it done.

While Dr Pepper enjoys nationwide distribution today, it was a regional drink for many years and originated in Waco, Texas. Carhops at drive-ins had a slang language, which they used when turning in an order. An order for a Dr Pepper was referred to as a "Waco," a Coca-Cola was a "shoot," and a chocolate malt was a "choc dust." Thus a carhop's order might sound like "shoot one, a Waco, and a choc dust." Their slang also referred to a hamburger with mayonnaise as a "sissy burger" since most folks in Texas preferred their burgers with mustard.

There were other variety programs that originated in Dallas. For many years WFAA broadcast the "Early Bird Show," which was aired early in the morning five days a week. They had a regular cast of characters and a band. "Hackberry Hotel" and "Little Willie" were two of the mainstays. This program originated from the refurbished facilities of the old University Club atop the No. 2 Unit of the Santa Fe Building. We never attended the "Early Bird Show," since it came on about the same time we had to leave for school.

Most radio programs employed an applause sign when they wanted the audience to clap, but Roy Cowan had a straw sailor hat, which had a rigid brim and a pillbox crown. They were widely used in vaudeville acts and by banjo players during the '20s. They were also standard apparel for men during the hot summer months.

The one Roy Cowan wore had been modified with a flashlight reflector in the front of the crown with batteries inside the hat. When he wanted the audience to applaud, he pressed a button and the light in front of the hat would give the signal for the audience to respond. All of the programs were wholesome and family oriented and enjoyed by all ages.

My mother had a rickety old treadle-operated Singer sewing machine on which she made all of her housedresses, aprons, and some of my shirts, as many women did back then.

A housedress was a very simple garment made of cotton fabric with little or no adornment. She had a cedar chest full of remnants that she had acquired over the years. When she would see an ad in one of the papers that told of a remnant sale at one of the department stores, she would get on the streetcar as soon as possible to get there before the doors opened. She had a technique for remnant shopping that was second to none. These sales were very popular and attended by a large number of women. My mother would work her way up to the table where the remnants were displayed and start sorting through the pile. She would pick up five or six pieces she was interested in buying, take them over to a corner out of the crowd where she could decide which ones she wanted.

After making her selections, she took the rest back to the table. The purchases then went into her inventory stored in the cedar chest. This common domestic talent went a long way in easing the financial burdens of store-bought clothes.

Most housewives had sewing machines, and many things came in reusable patterned cloth sacks. This included sugar and flour, and also animal feeds and seeds. My Aunt Dorothy used to make Cousin Harry's underwear out of Domino sugar sacks, and when asked what was on his underwear, being too little to pronounce "Domino," he would say "Nominee," which was the best he could manage.

Present generations don't realize how frugal people had to be to exist. There was so little money in circulation prior to the massive government spending required for rearmament prior to World War II.

When it came to sales, there was none better than the "Ridiculous Sale," which was held annually by Dreyfus & Sons men's clothiers. They were merchants for men's fine apparel, and they offered boy's clothes at truly ridiculously low prices. My mother watched the paper each year for the event and would take me on the streetcar to town to the sale. Sometimes there was very little available in my size, but when there was, I enjoyed the luxury of truly fine clothes that we could not otherwise afford.

Each year we would encounter Mrs. Engle at the sale. She had three boys for whom she shopped. Her husband, "Pop" Engle, operated a used car lot and wrecking yard on Main Street, where in 1937 I bought my first car.

Her son Herb was approximately my age, and in later years, he took over his dad's business that had been converted from used cars to the auto glass business. The auto glass business was very successful. They had several outlets, and later Herb sold out to a large glass company and remained inactive for a number of years as per the agreement with the purchaser. After the required non-competitive period, his son Dennis returned to the business, and Pop Engle Glass Company survives to this day.

Pop Engle and Sons

Before Herb passed away, he and I enjoyed reminiscing about which of us was the poorest while we were growing up. He even denied having any clothing from Dreyfus & Sons, but my memory was better than his and I knew that he did.

Herb loved to tell the story that when we went to high school we were summoned to the auditorium with all of the other new male students. That is where we were given the opportunity to take ROTC, but were told that we would have to buy a pair of military shoes.

Herb stated that this was why he declined ROTC because his family could not afford to buy him military shoes. My retort to this was that my mother felt that if the school was going to furnish the uniform to wear four days a week and that she had to buy me shoes anyway, this presented an ideal situation.

However, I was told not to do so well in military that I would be promoted to an officer status, since officers had to buy their own uniforms and a saber. She felt that this was an unnecessary expense, so I dutifully followed her instructions and I never rose above corporal.

It was approximately 1935 when my father started teaching me to drive. Since he didn't own a car at that time he would borrow his sister Viola's 1934 Chevrolet and we would drive out to White Rock Lake where he would allow me to take over.

But first I would have to raise the driver's bucket seat and put a piece of 2x4 under it. This would allow me to see over the steering wheel. I was only 12 years old and small for my age.

This was the beginning of my love affair with both White Rock Lake and automobiles. I had always enjoyed riding around the lake, but this was my first experience at the wheel.

As 1935 drew to a close, I was filled with anticipation of being promoted to junior high school. In January 1936 I bade farewell to Mt. Auburn grade school and was promoted to seventh grade at J. L. Long Jr. High school.

It was a relatively new school at that time and possessed the latest educational equipment, which included a metal shop, a wood shop, and an excellent science lab. It had been built on the campus adjoining Woodrow Wilson High School. I elected to take metal shop where the students were taught how to do aluminum casting, metal turning, steel forming, and welding, both electric and gas.

The wood shop taught wood turning, carpentry and furniture fabrication. These were valuable lessons for students who were not planning to go on to college. The science lab was well equipped and the course included general science and astronomy.

The principal at J. L. Long Jr. High School served a dual roll in that he was principal there as well as at Mt. Auburn. All the women teachers during my entire schooling were either single or widowed, since the Dallas Independent School District had a rule prohibiting married female teachers. This practice was commonplace due to the fact that a married woman was expected to be supported by her husband, and a single woman was in greater need of the job.

The school enrollment grew to such an extent that portable classrooms were also required at J. L. Long. I suppose it is almost impossible to predict the student growth in the public school system from year to year, as even today, portable classrooms are much in evidence at most major schools.

We took great pride in J. L. Long since it had many amenities not possessed by Mt. Auburn grade school. The auditorium was large, with theater type seating, and the more modern, well-equipped cafeteria was a great improvement.

The gymnasium was huge, with a wall down the middle to divide the boys and girls. As mentioned before, the shops and science lab had the latest equipment.

These days, if a thermometer is broken at school and a minute amount of mercury is spilled, an emergency is declared, and the school is closed for the day while the area is decontaminated. This contrasts greatly with the jug of mercury in the science lab at J. L. Long. It was about the size of a one-pound coffee can and was about half full of mercury.

Some students would coat pennies with it and try to pass them as dimes in the cafeteria. It was played with, with little concern, and I know of no serious consequences resulting from this practice.

In 1934, the cost of movies was 25 cents for matinees and 50 cents for the evenings for the downtown theaters, with children's admissions a dime. Most neighborhood theaters charged 25 cents for adults and 10 cents for children. Many of them had only washed air, which was better than nothing, but not much.

To stimulate business during the week, many neighborhood theaters featured "dish night," at which time they gave a piece of "Depression Ware" glass plates, cups and saucers, and serving dishes, to all who attended. These items are much sought after and costly today in antique stores.

In 1935 the American Petroleum Institute had their national convention in Dallas. This was the year that the Magnolia Petroleum Company erected the revolving flying red horse on top of the Magnolia Building. It remained there until 1999 when it was removed for restoration and new illumination that outlined the horse in neon tube lighting.

It was replaced in all of its glory for the new millennium celebration in 2000. The Magnolia building has been converted from an office building to a luxury hotel and is situated directly across Akard Street from the Adolphus Hotel, which has been completely renovated and modernized as well.

An enclosed walkway was constructed above Commerce Street from the Adolphus to the Baker Hotel directly across the street. This was for the convenience of the conventioneers. It was subsequently removed, but many enclosed overhead walkways have been constructed in downtown Dallas in later years.

Another highlight of the Saturday morning trip to town was the chance to go to the top of the Magnolia building for an unobstructed view of the entire city. This was done by riding one of the elevators to the top floor of the building, and then climbing two flights of stairs to the observation tower, which was immediately below Pegasus the flying red horse.

The entire observation deck was enclosed with chain link fencing so it could not be used as a suicide jump-off, which had been the case at the Tower Petroleum Building and the Hilton Hotel, and doubtless others.

One Saturday I took my little cousin Harry, who was about

six, to town to go to the top of the building. I was wearing my pith (or jungle) helmet, of which I was very proud. When we got to the observation deck I decided to tease him a little and told him, "I think I'll jump off." And without a moment's hesitation he said, "Well, can I have your jungle helmet before you jump?"

Back then, kids under 12 could ride to town on the streetcar for three cents, see a movie at any one of the numerous downtown theaters for 10 cents, and ride back home for the total sum of 16 cents. We didn't have extra money for popcorn, candy, and soft drinks.

In the 1920s, Dallas was linked to Oak Cliff by the Houston Street viaduct, which was the longest concrete bridge in the world when it was built. After the levees along the Trinity River were constructed subsequent to the straightening of the channel, a series of new viaducts were built.

The one now referred to as the Commerce Street viaduct was initially accessible by crossing a steel automotive bridge that spanned the railroad tracks at the foot of Main Street. This bridge was later eliminated by the construction of the Triple Underpass, which allowed Main, Elm, and Commerce to converge just west of the rail yards, where you then ascended to the viaduct just as you do today.

These three streets were illuminated by ground level lighting contained in kiosks on each side of the street. The citizens thought that this was a great step forward in modernizing Dallas, and most everyone wanted to go downtown to see this "engineering marvel."

I remember our family climbing into Uncle Harry's Pierce-Arrow for the inspection tour. A short time after the underpass opened, many people complained about an intensive glare from the grade level lighting. Upon closer inspection, it was discovered that the reflectors in the fixtures were installed upside down, which caused the lights to shine upward into the eyes of the motorists instead of downward on the pavement.

One of my most anticipated and enjoyed activities was going downtown by streetcar on Saturday morning. This event was very similar in nature to youngsters going to the mall today.

I would peruse all the five and dime stores, usually buying very little, but it was a place of wonderment, especially Grand Silver Company, which was on the ground floor of the Wilson Building in the space later occupied by H. L. Greene.

They carried such things as electric bells used as doorbells, dry cell batteries and flashlights, and rubber half soles, which had adhesive on the backside that you could apply to the bottom of your shoes if you had worn out the soles.

I knew some boys who would apply them to brand new shoes so they would not wear out the soles. They also carried rubber heels for men's shoes that you could apply yourself. They had a shoe repair department, as did many of the stores in that day, including some of the department stores. They were equipped with little waist-high stalls where you could sit and remove your shoes and have them repaired while you waited.

Many men and boys had only one pair of shoes. Along those same lines, the local dry cleaners also offered a pressing service that could be carried out while you waited.

There were many small "mom and pop" grocery stores scattered throughout Dallas. They handled the kind of items now found in 7-11 stores, and some of the stores in the better neighborhoods had a small meat market.

Not many families had an automobile and those who did had only one car, which was not always at the housewife's disposal. The housewife could walk to the neighborhood store or send one of the children if she needed the usual staples.

I used to ride my bicycle to Mrs. Snell's or Mrs. Florence's store for a loaf of bread or a can of something. The attraction for me, however, being a life-long sweets lover, was that all of these stores had a display filled to the brim with a vast array of penny candies — like Tootsie Rolls, Chocolate Soldiers, jawbreakers, Fleer's Double-Bubble gum, as well as licorice rope.

Most families did a weekly shopping trip to a Safeway, A&P, or Piggly Wiggly to restock their cupboards, since prices at the major grocers were considerably less than the smaller neighborhood stores.

The A&P Stores had a wonderful aroma, since they sold two brands of coffee, Eight-O-Clock and Bokar, which were sold in bean form in sacks and they were ground for you at the checkout counter. Cookies from National Biscuit Company (now NABISCO) were stocked in large factory boxes with a hinged glass front, and it rested in a rack that kept the box tilted back so the cookies wouldn't fall on the floor when the door was opened. Customers reached in and bagged the desired quantity.

Dried beans came in small sealed paper bags that had a glassine window so that the size and type of bean could be seen by the shopper.

Chapter Five

1934 CHICAGO CENTURY OF PROGRESS

1934 was a very eventful year, as it was that summer that we made a trip to Prairie du Chien, Wisconsin to visit my great-grandmother.

Her grandson Al Jr. was slightly younger than I, and we whiled away the summer hours hunting for Indian arrowheads, which had, in years past, been quite plentiful since this was the area of the Blackhawk Indian wars.

The town was the site of a former military fort. We also would place pennies on the railroad track, which was about a block behind my great-grandmother's house, and watch the locomotives flatten them out.

One day we decided to see what the engine would do in the way of flattening a large wood screw that we placed on the track. Much to our surprise, as the train approached, we noted that the train was actually going backwards and the lighter weight caboose came first. When it ran over the screw, it scared us to death because it made an awful racket and we were afraid it was going to derail.

It was on these rails that one day the Burlington Railroad stationed a man at each railroad/street crossing in the city, this in anticipation of a very fast train making its inaugural run. Al Jr. and I stood near the tracks in hopes of seeing this phenomenon. Much to our disappointment, the famous Burlington Zephyr came roaring in at the amazing speed of about 15 miles per hour. It must have been ahead of schedule. This train is now on display at the Museum of Science and Industry in Chicago.

One afternoon, while he and I were lying on the grass looking at the clouds and talking of different things, I made a statement, the nature of which I don't remember, but he said to me, "You lie." His accusation infuriated me greatly and I punched him in the nose. Blood went everywhere and he went hollering in the house and I was in trouble with his mother and grandmother.

My mother staunchly defended me, saying he had no right to call me a liar. Later that day I was next door at our uncle's house, and he seemed pleased at the news, since I gathered that Al Jr. was a spoiled kid and he got what he deserved.

On our return trip from Wisconsin, we stopped off at Chicago to visit my mother's Aunt Otilia, her husband, Sigward, and their son John. While in Chicago we visited the 1934 Century of Progress Worlds Fair. I was nearly 12 years old and had hoped to spend a great deal more time at the Fair than we did. But in spite of my short visit, it made a great impression, and I saw many things that were of interest to me.

The fair had two very tall steel towers that were accessible by elevator, and we took the trip to the top of one. From there you could see into three states: Illinois, Indiana, and Wisconsin. About midway up the towers were enclosed trams much the size and configuration of a city bus, which you could ride from one tower to the other and back again. They all were named after characters in the famous "Amos 'n' Andy" radio program. We chose not to take this ride since a previous equipment failure had stranded all of them for the better part of the day, and we could hardly take the chance of it happening to us.

The fairground was built on an island created by dredging Lake Michigan and depositing the material to build a man-made island.

My cousin and I toured the large wooden ship used as an icebreaker by Admiral Byrd on his first Antarctic expedition.

We also visited numerous buildings, among them the Hall of Transportation, which was a unique structure in that the roof was supported by exterior bracing, creating a clear span on the interior of the building.

There were many villages representing numerous countries. And while the fair was titled Century of Progress, it was truly international in flavor and was referred to as a "Worlds Fair."

Virtually all American manufacturers were represented at the fair. The exposition ran during summer months from 1933 to 1934.

And while Ford Motor Company was not represented in 1933, General Motors exhibited an assembly line where they assembled 1933 Chevrolets, and orders placed in advance were delivered to buyers at the fair. I think that this convinced Mr. Ford that his company should be represented for the 1934 year.

They constructed a big round building that was designed to look like two very large gears stacked one on top of the other. It was called "The Rotunda" and was moved to Dearborn, Michigan after the fair. It served the Ford Motor Company for many years until a fire damaged it beyond repair.

One of the main Midway attractions was fan dancer Sally Rand, much the same way that Little Egypt was the main attraction at the 1893 Columbian Exposition also held in Chicago. Then in 1934, she appeared with big bubbles as her prop rather than the fans from the previous year.

Ms. Rand also appeared two years later with Billy Rose at the Frontier Centennial Exposition in Fort Worth, Texas with her show entitled the "Nude Ranch."

While at the fair in Chicago, I purchased a little viewer that contained a filmstrip of 35mm black and white photos showing the various buildings and attractions. It is in my collection of memorabilia and is still in good working order. It was truly a marvelous exposition.

At the close of our visit to Chicago, we went to the downtown bus station in order to catch a dilapidated old bus operated by the Golden Eagle Line. From all appearances their coaches were well-worn former Greyhound Line busses, and a fleet of them had been assembled to run excursions to the Worlds Fair at a very nominal price.

As was the custom, all the passengers' luggage was loaded on top of the bus and covered with a tarp in case of rain. The old bodies were so loose that with the weight of the luggage on the top that the side walls would flex and lean when you went around a corner.

One of the rest stops on the way home was the Keystone Hotel in Joplin, Missouri. When we all unloaded off the bus, the driver lifted the hood on the right side and it was evident that he had a rather serious gasoline leak out of the vacuum tank, which was used to pull gasoline up from the rear mounted fuel tank to the engine.

These were widely used on cars and trucks, and were later replaced by fuel pumps. We all got back on the bus, but when the driver attempted to start it, the engine caught fire. This caused immediate panic on the part of many of the passengers, all of whom were trying to get out of the only door on the bus.

A woman directly behind me kept saying, "Everybody keep calm. Everybody stay calm," but in her haste she pushed me over

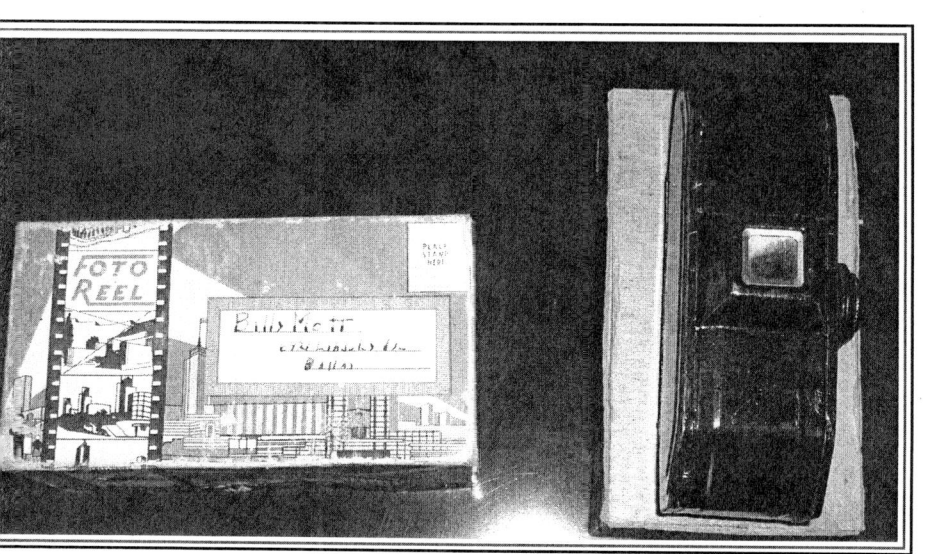

Filmstrip viewer from the 1934 Chicago Exposition

into the front seat, which enabled me to get out of the door. After some tightening and adjusting, the driver restarted the engine, and we were allowed to board the bus and resume our journey. It had been a very dry year and was responsible for the dust bowl in Oklahoma.

But as we proceeded toward Texas from Missouri, a torrential rain occurred for which everyone was grateful, but the bus passengers were afraid to shut the windows in case there was a recurrence of the fire and it would be a means of escape. Needless to say, everyone got quite wet as the rain poured in, but no one seemed to mind.

Compared to today's jet travel, this would seem very primitive.

Chapter Six

HIGH SCHOOL YEARS

In January of 1938 I was promoted frcm J. L. Long to Woodrow Wilson High School, which at that time was only one of six high schools serving Dallas, and was the newest in the Dallas School system.

I continued to do vacuum cleaner and appliance repair to earn my spending money. Money was still very scarce, and if I had an opportunity to install some light fixtures or do electrical repairs, my mother would allow me to play hooky from school in order to earn the extra money.

In ROTC all cadets were urged to gc to Camp Dallas, a military type summer camp near Mineral Wells. This was supposed to assure you of a more rapid promotion in ROTC. This was not an enticement for me, since I had already been informed by my mother that she could not afford my promotion.

Woodrow Wilson High School had the largest ROTC Corp in the U.S., and it numbered over 600 cadets. The Cadet Corp had early morning parades on the football field on regular occasions. On those days we had to be at school extremely early in order to complete the parade before class time started.

Some people can sing "I Love A Parade," but my mother said she hated the parade since she had to get up so early to fix my breakfast. In addition to the parades, each afternoon when school was dismissed at 3:15 a flag detail would lower the flag while a trumpeter played Retreat, and if you were still on school property, you were required to face the flag, and if you were in ROTC uniform you had to salute until the flag was lowered.

I was able to get occasional public opinion survey work through Mrs. Gaines, who was in the advertising business, and received contracts to do public opinion surveys. My mother and father also worked on these surveys, and since my mother never drove a car, she had to depend on public transportation and sometimes had to travel by interurban to Denton and Terrell.

On September 1, 1939 Adolph Hitler ordered the invasion of Poland. While everyone was concerned and distressed, few realized the enormous impact this action would have on the world.

Everyone hoped the U.S. would not be involved, but as soon as England and France declared war on Germany as a result of treaties with Poland, most Americans realized the probability of our involvement. The U.S. was ill prepared to fight a war, as we had studied in ROTC that Congress had been unwilling to appropriate the money for a strong defense. President Roosevelt subsequently embarked on an ambitious national defense program, which would include the immediate production of 50,000 aircraft. This signaled the beginning of our rearmament program, and with the massive armament spending, would ultimately overcome our long period of economic depression.

Aircraft factories and ship building yards were built or expanded and thousands of people were put to work. This took place while our civilian economy continued to produce automobiles, stoves, refrigerators, and household appliances.

January 1941 saw my long anticipated graduation take place. I was almost late for my commencement exercise since I had worked from early that morning until late afternoon helping my dad install new light fixtures and some additional electrical outlets in a house that belonged to my step-grandmother, Grace.

She had purchased the house immediately after WW I and had rented it out for many years, but she and my grandfather had decided to ask the tenants to move so that they could remodel the house prior to moving into it.

My mother was very put out with my dad because he had used

up my entire day on the job, and I barely had time to bathe and dress before going to the commencement.

And not only that, but he had borrowed money from Grace and used the payment for our work to repay her. Consequently, I received nothing for a long day's work..

I had been most eager to own an automobile, and my mother agreed to give me $25 if I wanted to buy an old jalopy instead of going to Camp Dallas.

That is when I purchased an 11-year-old Model T Ford from Pop Engle. This proved to be a costly endeavor, as I spent most of my time repairing it. However, the experience proved to be a priceless benefit.

In spite of this first venture into car ownership, it was the beginning of a lifetime love of automobiles. When I was given the $25, my father was not living at home since it was one of his numerous separations from my mother.

I was pretty much on my own when it came to negotiating the purchase of a car. A couple of my friends agreed to accompany me on my excursion downtown to shop for a $25 automobile.

Auto Row, as it was known in those days, was located on Main Street on the eastern fringe of the central business district. The purpose for this was primarily because several streetcar lines converged at the eastern end of Main Street and followed it downtown. This allowed streetcar riders to view the dealers' inventories as they rode to and from work.

My friends and I got off the streetcar near downtown and started visiting the car lots as we headed east on Main Street. Even in those depression days we found very few autos available for $25 or less. I had already determined that I could not pay more than $25 cash, since I had no steady source of income and would not be able to make monthly payments.

I knew that if the car was paid for and I didn't have money to buy gas for it, it would just have to sit at home. Public liability insurance was not required and very few people carried it due to the added expense. It was an entirely different world in the '30s. It is hard to realize today that people did not feel it was necessary. Lawsuits were very rare, and folks settled their differences amiably.

After shopping almost the full length of Auto Row, I spied a 1927 Model T Ford coupe, which had a homemade type rumble seat in it. I went in Pop Engle's little office and asked him the price. When he told me it was $25, I was elated, since it did fit my budget exactly. He told one of his workmen to start it for me so that I might hear it run. This was most unusual and gracious on his part, inasmuch as most of the dealers I had visited would scarcely give me the time of day since I was only 15 years old at the time.

I had always aspired to own a Model T Ford, as high school boys for many generations drove Model T Fords to school if they had a car at all. Pop Engle asked me if I knew how to drive a Model T Ford, and I told him yes, but I had never driven one since my learning to drive had all been done on standard shift cars.

But I knew that a Model T was simpler to drive than a stick shift and I had no hesitancy to give it a try. A Model T Ford had three pedals, with the one on the extreme left being low gear when fully depressed and high gear when fully released, giving you only two forward speeds. The reverse pedal was in the center, and to back up you pressed the low-high pedal halfway down with your left foot and then pressed the reverse pedal with your right foot. There was no accelerator pedal, because a lever on the steering column controlled the throttle. This freed both feet for the pedal work.

When my friends and I returned home, I think the whole neighborhood turned out to see my new acquisition. It created as much excitement as if someone had come home in a new Packard or Cadillac. Many of the other mothers thought my mother had taken leave of her senses to let a 15-year-old boy buy an automobile. Little did they know there was a method to her madness in that she did not drive a car and in my father's absence had no means of getting about since Harry and Dorothy had also moved out.

As I look back on my experience, the Model T was no bargain, as some previous owner had reassembled the engine using pieces of a corrugated box as an oil pan gasket. This so-called economy move allowed it to leak oil very badly, but the old Ford was dependable, and I put many miles on it for about two years.

I made an agreement with the two boys who I took to school and back each day that they would buy me one gallon of gas per week for the service. Gasoline was only 11 and 12 cents a gallon, and while the father of one of the boy's was very wealthy, he was very poor pay and I would have to ask him for payment after two or three weeks.

One of our summer activities was to get in the Ford and go to what we called the junkyard. It consisted of a large depression, or ditch, just off of Dolphin Road and Haskell Avenue. A black man owned the property and he allowed car dealers and wrecking yards to dump old car bodies into the hole.

We would go out there and climb all over these discarded bodies, some of which had parking lights, chrome ornaments, door handles, or body parts which I could attach to the Model T. He only charged a few cents for anything you might want to buy, and we thought it to be great fun.

Later, when World War II occurred, he was able to sell every piece of scrap metal on the premises for the war effort.

We would also climb into the Model T and go swimming at the White Rock swimming beach or the Fair Park swimming pool, which was located just inside the Grand Avenue entrance to Fair Park.

Following one of their reconciliations, my dad, having no means of transportation and knowing my ability to repair appliances, suggested that he, as an adult, would solicit appliance repairs and I could furnish transportation. We agreed to split all of the profits.

It worked satisfactorily and we soon branched out into refrigeration repair as well as appliances. In that era, household refrigerators had belt-driven compressors and used sulphur-dioxide as a refrigerant. I had learned how to replace compressor seals, add refrigerant, and replace faulty floats or expansion valves as the case may be.

I vividly recall one repair job that we did in an upstairs apartment on Llano St. to an old Majestic refrigerator. We told the owners that in the condition it was in that it would not last very long, and since we knew a man who handled used refrigerators, we agreed to work out a deal where they would trade in their balky Majestic on a much later model Servel electric.

It was a very nice looking box and the dealer had it operating in his store. He said that the only problem with it was that it tended to kick out the circuit breaker occasionally, but he had wired around it. Arrangements were made, the Servel was delivered and set up in the apartment, and we assumed we had their problem solved.

This euphoria was short lived, since we received a call that same afternoon that the Servel had caught fire, and the Fire Department had to be called to put out the blaze. We were greatly relieved to find out that the customer carried insurance, and the insurance company paid for a new refrigerator. To me it was a beautiful example of divine providence.

The Model T Ford continued to serve as a work vehicle, but it was getting very tired and antiquated. On one occasion while driving down Oram Street the rear axle broke, and since a Model T's braking system was in the transmission, it left me with no brakes.

The axle broke near the center of the car, and as it worked its way out, it let the axle housing down on the ground. The broken axle required the services of a wrecker to take the car to our house.

For some time I had been aware of a Model T sedan parked on Collett Street directly across from Lindy's Tavern. It had been sitting there so long that the top, which was fabric, had collapsed into the passenger compartment. I talked to Mr. Lindburg, who said he was the owner and had used it for deliveries in the past, and he agreed to sell it to me for $10.

I planned to change out the entire rear axle assembly in order to put my Ford back on the road. I had a friend take me down to pick up my new purchase. I took along the battery out of my Ford, along with some gasoline.

Upon starting the car I found that the engine ran very smooth and much quieter than the one in my coupe. An additional bonus was that the engine didn't leak any oil. Needless to say, I was thrilled with my purchase and immediately began work on transplanting the entire running gear into my original car. After removing all usable parts from the sedan, we hauled the body and frame out into the country and dumped it into a convenient gully.

After a divorce, my Aunt Dorothy decided to remarry. The man lived in Athens, Texas, and my mother, Harry Jr., and I made plans to attend the wedding. I decided to drive my Model T. My mother declined to accept a ride and elected to go by bus, feeling that it was a more appropriate mode of transportation, and allowed her to make a dignified arrival.

Looking back, it was a little unusual to allow a 15-year-old boy to take his seven-year-old cousin on an 80-mile trip in a Model T Ford.

Ironically, the Model T made the round trip to the wedding without incident, but the Dixie Trailways bus bearing my mother broke down on the trip, much to her chagrin, delaying her arrival in Athens by several hours. Thank goodness the wedding was the next day.

Since I was now in my teenage years, and my appliance repair work did not supply a steady source of income with which to maintain an automobile and provide spending money, I decided to overcome this shortfall of cash by accepting a *Dallas Morning News* paper route.

The route I had was down around the Ford assembly plant and many of my customers were employed by Ford. Times were still very hard, and when the Ford plant was shut down due to lack of sales or a model changeover, it made collecting for a newspaper very difficult, since subscribers would have no income during this period.

Many times they would move out during the night, owing milk bills, paperboys, and utilities and rent. The newspapers had an arrangement with the utility companies and they would notify the paper carriers of any new utility turn-ons on their route. However, they refused to give us any information as to where any of our move-outs had relocated.

At that time there were several newspapers in Dallas, only one of which was a morning paper. Since my route was the *Dallas Morning News*, it was necessary for me to get up very early in order to throw my route before school. As I look back, I consider my paper route as a very unsatisfactory and frustrating experience, and perhaps the only endeavor in my life that I do not consider a success.

I began to feel the need of a more modern car for use in delivering the *Dallas Morning News,* a well as operating my appliance repair business. My funds were still quite limited and I feared that if I bought a car on which I would have to make monthly payments, I might not be able to handle it.

I found a little 1934 Plymouth two-door sedan sitting on the car lot of C. S. Hamilton Motor Company, the only Chrysler-Plymouth dealership in Dallas. I had saved up some money and I asked my father, who happened to be living at home at that time, to go with me to help negotiate the purchase. Since most adults were reluctant to do business with a minor, I felt his presence would carry weight.

As it turned out, one of the used car salesmen for the company was a gentleman named Dick Parker, who was a brother to George Parker, who was our next door neighbor on Summit Avenue. They were asking $125 for the car, but my dad told them that $50 was all I had, whereupon Dick Parker went to his boss and he accepted the offer.

The little Plymouth was well worn and had high mileage, but was a great improvement over the 1927 Ford. I was most elated to have a better car. During the three years I owned it I overhauled the engine, replaced the clutch and transmission, and repainted it with a borrowed air compressor, all in the backyard.

My two friends continued to ride to school with me for the price of one gallon of gas per week. I would occasionally take two sisters to school. They were Jean and Virginia Connolly, who lived around the corner on Newell Ave. I was really crestfallen the first time I picked them up in my new possession and Virginia said that she liked the Model T better.

During the summer of 1940, Walter Hunt, Al Smith, and yours truly decided we wanted to take a camping trip. Walter had a tent large enough to accommodate four cots, so we tied its center pole to the side of the car and loaded everything else inside and headed for Sulphur, Oklahoma.

At that time, what is now known as Federal Recreation Area was then called the Platt National Park. We had heard good things about it so we were off on our adventure. We experienced no trouble whatsoever with the car and upon arrival we picked out one of the designated camping sites and erected our tent and then struck out to explore the park.

There are a number of natural springs, some of which contained various minerals, as well as a flowing brook and some wooded hills, which made a very picturesque place to visit.

It was an awfully hot summer, and after a couple of nights there we were ready to break camp and head home. Can't say it was a lot cooler at home, but at least we had an electric fan and an electric refrigerator.

This was my first camping experience, and to the best of my recollection, my last. My idea of roughing it is a Holiday Inn with black and white TV.

I greatly enjoyed having a more modern car, but I had not addressed the problem of disposing of the Model T Ford. I was now the proud owner of two automobiles, consisting of a total investment of only $75. I let it be known at the little two pump gas station where I traded that I wanted to sell the Model T. Since it had had an engine transplant as well as a replacement differential, it was a pretty good car, as far as Model T's go.

One day as I was repairing a refrigerator during the summer, my mother had a visitor. He was a man referred by the service station who wanted to see the Ford I had for sale. My mother told him to look it over, that it was in the backyard, and that I would be home later in the afternoon so he could discuss it and test-drive it.

I was really excited to know that I had a prospective buyer and anxiously awaited his return after I finished working. When he showed up, he told me that his name was Ted Evers, and that he had been working in California as a dishwasher for several months, and had saved up some money, which he carried in a money belt. He had wanted to return to Atlanta, Texas to visit his mother, and attempt to find work there.

Times were still quite hard and the nation's rearmament program had not as yet helped the employment situation. He told me that he had gone to California and returned by riding in boxcars on the railroad, and that on his return from California he never let any of the other hobos know that he had any money whatsoever on his person.

After looking over the Ford and giving it a test drive, he said that he would pay my asking price of $50 if I would install a new set of bands in the transmission. I agreed to do this, since it was something I had done several times since I owned the car.

I had to pay to have the first set installed, but I watched as the mechanic did the job and from that point forward I knew how to do it myself. He came back the next day and paid me the $50. While this was $25 more than I had paid for the car, it was in much better condition than when I first bought it.

I had kept the old worn-out engine in the garage, and told him he could have it whenever he wanted it. I didn't see him again for several weeks, but one morning, before 6:00, there was a knock on the door, and there stood Ted Evers, who said he had come to pick up the engine. I guess he thought he could use it for spare parts, or that it had some value if he wanted to sell it. He stated that he was on his way back to California, since the only employment he could find in Atlanta, Texas was selling fish out of an ice container in the back of the Model T.

My mother thought that was certainly an ignominious end for such a nice little car. We told Mr. Evers that he would have to wait until at least 7:30 before we could allow him to create the racket associated with loading up the spare engine. He dutifully waited in front of the house until the appointed time, and then backed down the driveway to the garage where he loaded the motor onto the rear bumper arms.

This was the last I ever saw of Mr. Evers as he headed for the Golden West.

Walter Hunt lived in a lovely two-story home on Tennison Memorial Drive. The Hunts had several wooded acres surrounding the house, which sat back from the road on a tree shaded gravel drive. The entrance had two large gates, which were closed each evening to enhance security. Mr. Hunt was a very successful insurance man. He had a hobby of raising chickens and had a large flock.

On occasion, he would invite all of Walter's friends to a

barbecue, where he would cook a number of chickens for us. We always enjoyed these parties, and in later years I was told by some of the girls who attended that that was the first time they had ever eaten barbecued chicken.

At one time, Mr. Hunt had a carpenter build a tree house for Walter, high up in one of the native pecan trees in the yard. It consisted of a platform that was totally enclosed in chicken wire. Access was through a trap door in the floor, and we spent the night in the tree house several times.

As a young boy, Walter was afflicted with a rather serious stutter. The Hunts made every effort to help him overcome this malady. One time they employed a speech therapist who had a machine that randomly displayed words which were to be repeated by the patient. In addition to this procedure, a later treatment required that he not speak at all for a specific period of time. Neither course of action seemed to produce the desired results. Walter eventually not only overcame his stuttering, but following World War II went into the ministry and became a missionary in the Philippines. He always credited the Lord with his recovery, and felt he had been called to serve in His name. He never stuttered when he was preaching.

During one very, very cold winter, I developed a really bad case of influenza. During this intense cold spell, while I was sick in bed, my father had to throw my *Dallas Morning News* route for me. He was able to get Billy Gaines, whose family lived in the small side of the Lindsley Ave. duplex, to go with him in the 1934 Plymouth each morning until I recovered sufficiently to resume my duties.

It was during this same winter that we heard that Walter Hunt was in the hospital with pneumonia. In those days pneumonia was a very serious illness, and a patient became progressively worse until they reached a fever crisis, whereupon they either got better or they died.

Al Smith and I decided to go see Walter one evening, and we went by and picked up the Connolly girls, who were distressed to hear of Walter's condition. We went down to a small hospital on Gaston Avenue, which was directly across from Baylor Hospital, and later became the Gaston Episcopal Hospital. We were told by the nurses that they were using a new sulfa drug on Walter, and that it was performing miracles for pneumonia patients.

After visiting Walter, who appeared to be on the mend, we stopped at Mrs. Baird's Bakery, which was then located on the corner of Bryan and Carroll Streets. It was a custom of the bakery to give tours at night to anyone who came in. They gave us a loaf of freshly baked unsliced bread, which we all shared on the way home. Since we had the girls with us, we called it a "cheap date."

Chapter Seven

LOWER GREENVILLE AVENUE

What is now considered Lower Greenville Avenue was one of Dallas' early suburban shopping centers. In the '20s the sidewalks were constructed of wooden planks. There were a variety of businesses up and down the street, including bakeries, barbecue stands, furniture stores, dry goods stores, Mr. Whorton's Magnolia gas station at the corner of Greenville and Alta, and the Arcadia Theater where they presented movies and vaudeville. It had a pipe organ, which was played by Jack Caldwell who was later to be an army buddy of mine.

In the '70s, the Greenville Avenue Bank made it a custom to bring in an electric organ at Christmas time and have Jack come in daily and play Christmas music. I was employed at the bank during the early '70s and thoroughly enjoyed Jack's music each Christmas season.

Another pleasant Greenville Ave. memory recalls the Weber's Root Beer stand on the corner of Greenville and Richmond Avenues, where for a nickel you could get a large frosty mug of root beer served in your car, and if you had children with you they received a small complimentary mug of root beer. Weber's Root Beer stands were prevalent throughout the city as were outdoor watermelon gardens where cold slices of watermelon were served at convenient

Lower Greenville Avenue during the "Roaring Twenties"

tables. Each of these enterprises provided a cooling respite from the summer heat.

Another treat around the corner on Oakland was the Dixie Cream Donut factory where you could always drop in for a fresh warm donut. Anytime was a good time for a Dixie Cream donut, which were considered the Krispy-Kreams of their day.

One of the founders and subsequent Chairman of the Board of the Greenville Avenue Bank, Charlie Wise, was a most colorful character. Charlie had begun his working career as a barber in a shop on the corner of Greenville and Oram Streets. He later moved to a shop in the Arcadia Theater building.

He took night courses at Dixie College, which was in the YMCA building on Commerce Street (later razed to provide the site for the new Statler-Hilton Hotel). He passed the bar exam and became a lawyer/barber and practiced law from then until his death in 1976. Everyone used to refer to him as "The Mayor of Greenville Avenue."

Lower Greenville Avenue

The barbershop was still in operation in 2002 under ownership of Bill Adams, who just recently closed the shop.

Up until May 31, 1999 one of the older establishments on Greenville was Charley Edward's National Cleaners, located at Greenville and LaVista. He was directly across the street from M. B. Kiser Heating and Air-conditioning Company, which was one of the pioneer companies in Dallas during the early years of air-conditioning.

You could often pass by the cleaners and see Charlie sitting in the front window of the shop where he operated an old treadle sewing machine, making alterations and putting in hems on men's pant legs. Like many long-time merchants, Charlie finally decided it was time to retire and go fishing. Unfortunately he enjoyed only three or four years before passing away in 2002. He, too, was known as the mayor of Greenville Avenue, inheriting the title after Charlie Wise passed away.

As do many self-made men, Melvin Kiser had started his business in a small wooden building near the corner of Elm Street at 2nd Ave. He told me many times that the business was started with $500 in capital and some hand tools. He was a man of great ability and built a large successful company that incorporated several departments, one of which was one of the best sheet metal shops in the area where they built all of the ductwork needed for the jobs.

While I was working at the Greenville Avenue Bank, my wife, Barbara, painted an oil picture of a sunrise over the desert for me, which I hung in my office. Melvin so admired it that Barbara painted one for him as well. It hung in the front window of the M. B. Kiser Company until the day it closed.

One of our favorite hangouts on lower Greenville Avenue was a well-known Italian restaurant named Sammy's. It was owned by Carlos Messina, and was built in 1932 by his uncle. It continued in operation under the Sammy's name until 1958, and became one of Dallas' "hot spots" during its heyday.

The restaurant could serve 66 people, and at one time employed 15 carhops to handle the drive-in customers in the lot out back that was capable of holding up to 40 cars and had its own separate kitchen on the back of the building. On Friday nights all of the school-aged kids would congregate there, and on Saturdays the young swinging singles in their 20s and 30s came in to eat. They didn't like sharing with the younger Friday night crowd.

Sammy's Italian Restaurant – Lower Greenville – 1932

Chapter Eight
EAST GRAND AVENUE

East Grand Avenue in front of Mt. Auburn Elementary School was paved just prior to my starting to school. In the fall of the year trucks loaded with cottonseed were a regular sight driving down the road from outlying gins. They were destined for cotton oil processing plants on the southern edge of town. This oil was used to make oleomargarine as well as cooking oil, and both sides of East Grand would be littered with the cottonseed that blew off of the trucks as they went past.

This stretch of East Grand was also utilized to test drive new Model A Fords that did not pass final inspection inside the plant, located a few blocks toward town from the school. The Ford plant was the major economic engine for the development of housing additions in the area. It was also the reason for the opening of the Grand Avenue State Bank in 1927 so that the employees would have a place to deposit or cash their paychecks.

Early on, Mr. Ford paid his employees in cash with $2 bills. This was so that the merchants and bankers would know from whence the money came.

Many of my schoolmates' fathers worked at the Ford plant. At that time the majority of people in East Dallas drove Fords, either because they or a member of their family was employed by Ford or because used Fords were very cheap. And prior to Ford becoming unionized, Mr. Ford specified that if his employees did not have a Ford when they went to work for him, the next car they bought would have to be a Ford product. Once organized, the union demanded this practice cease.

Because of the scarcity of money, people were all interested in free entertainment. By this time most people had radios, and "Major Bowes' Amateur Hour" was a very popular program nationwide. In light of its popularity, the merchants of the East Grand shopping district in East Dallas very near the Ford plant decided to sponsor an amateur hour of local talent. The show was conducted on a small stage that had been constructed in Samuels Park next door to the fire station, located at East Grand Avenue and Beacon Street.

On the summer nights when the amateur hour was held, attendance was high, and anyone able to exhibit any kind of talent was urged to participate. This continued for several years during the summer until times improved and people preferred to go to a cool movie house in preference to anything outdoors. However, there were a number of baseball diamonds in Samuels Park and a lot of people went to see the girl's baseball teams compete at night.

At both of these events, as well as on the neighborhood streets, the Good Humor man was always present. These vendors had a number of bells mounted above the windshields of their trucks that they jingled to announce their approach. This was before the advent of recorded music on ice cream trucks. When the children heard the bells, they began to beg their mothers for nickels to buy treats.

My friend Al Smith always paid for his ice cream with an empty milk bottle, which carried a five-cent deposit on it, and the ice cream man was willing to take milk bottles in exchange for a treat. I wonder if some sort of deposit system would work today to cut down on the tremendous drink can problem. It's true that a lot of people do recycle, but a little rebate would be a great incentive.

During those hot summer days of 1934 it was very difficult to get relief from the extreme heat. Businesses as well as many homes had canvas awnings on the windows to provide shade. Commercial buildings had awnings across the front that could be let down over the sidewalk, thus shading their front windows. This operation was accomplished by a little gear box mounted on the front of the building and was operated by the proprietor, who placed a little crank into the gear box and cranked the awning down in the morning and up in the evening. There was very little air-conditioning in retail stores and barbershops and grocery stores. Most of the movie houses had to have some form of cooling in order to lure in the customers. Some of them used what was called washed air, later known as evaporative cooling, but most of the big movie houses downtown in Dallas had refrigerated air by then.

Chapter Nine

1936 TEXAS CENTENNIAL

The most anticipated event in 1936 had to be the Texas Centennial Exposition, which was to be held in Dallas to commemorate Texas' independence from Mexico in 1836.

As early as 1903 the then governor of Texas, James Hogg, expressed hope that Texas could observe the 100th anniversary of the state's independence with statewide celebrations. Later, in the early '20s, a survey committee mailed 10,000 questionnaires to prominent citizens of Texas to obtain their opinions on the idea of an exposition. The response to the questionnaire amounted to 60% of the mailings being returned with a majority in favor of an exposition.

While the year 1936 was still a long way off, an undertaking of this size would require an enormous amount of planning and discussion, not to mention financing. A great deal of discussion was held in the Texas House and Senate, with very little progress, and with the onset of the depression of 1929, strong public support for a centennial was lacking.

By 1934 Texas lawmakers realized that time was of the essence, since what had seemed a long time off in the future was really getting very close. Most of the major cities in Texas were competing for the privilege of holding the exposition. Houston felt that it should be held on the San Jacinto Battleground, the place where Texas' independence was won. Of course San Antonio, with the Alamo being considered the actual birthplace of Texas independence, felt they should have the privilege. And Austin, the State Capitol, believed that it was only a natural choice. The city of Dallas already possessed a large exposition site in the form of the grounds of the State Fair of Texas, and also wanted to be in the running.

It was ultimately decided that all of the cities wishing to be considered should bid on the privilege, and in addition to their monetary bid should supply a complete listing of the property proposed, along with a current value appraisal of the same. All bids were to be presented by September 1, 1934.

R. L. Thornton, who was then president of the Dallas Chamber of Commerce, was ready to accept the challenge. He held a meeting of all of the major retailers and oil companies of Dallas. He told them not to send any of their junior executives, but only the head men of the corporations who had the authority to make decisions. As a result, the business and civic leaders quickly endorsed the proposed bid and pledged their company's support as well as their own personal endorsement.

The outcome was that the State Fair grounds was proposed as a base, with additional acreage yet to be acquired included. This would ultimately amount to approximately 200 acres. Municipal bonds in the amount of three million dollars were approved with local businesses pledging an additional two million dollars. The Texas Centennial Commission, after reviewing all bids, awarded the exposition to Dallas since their bid was almost twice that of the next highest bid.

By late 1934 and early 1935, little progress had been made on construction due to delays in financing and plan approval. As late as May 1936 there was still much to do, and 6,000 men were employed to work in three shifts around the clock in order to be ready for the grand opening on June 6, 1936. Miraculously, the turnstiles were ready to click on June 6, but many of the buildings were as yet not totally completed.

As young boys, my friends and I were privileged to tour the grounds on a Saturday morning in early May. This was possible because our friend Wallace Whisnand's father, Bert, was a security officer at the grounds. He took us to work with him one morning in his car and let us out inside the gates, which were closed to the public. We spent a good part of the day looking at all of the activities going on and enjoying a preview look at the exposition. We would have stayed longer, but a uniformed security man confronted us and wanted to know how we gained entrance. He said he didn't care who let us in, but he was going to let us out, which he did.

President Roosevelt was originally to have officially opened the Centennial on June 6, 1936, but more important commitments necessitated delaying his trip to Dallas until the following Saturday, June 13. He appointed Daniel C. Roper to conduct the opening ceremonies on his behalf.

As a 13-year-old boy I had been anxiously waiting for this day, and came through the Grand Avenue gate that morning prior to the official opening. With Roosevelt's appearance due the following Saturday, the Secret Service had been told to locate a suitable open phaeton automobile with running boards to accommodate Secret Service men for the occasion. By 1936 cars of that type were no longer in production, but the Dallas fire chief, Rod Gamble, used a 1931 Packard seven-passenger phaeton, which belonged to the city.

Since the car was bright red and not proper for a presidential carriage, it was taken to R. C. "Buddy" Lambeth's body shop at 2708 Main Street, where it was repainted black for the occasion. I rode from the end of the Mt. Auburn streetcar line to First Avenue and Oak, where I was privileged to see the president, his wife, Eleanor, and his son James, accompanied by Governor James Allred, pass by on their way to the gate in front of the Music Hall.

The next day, Sunday, June 7, our family drove out to Lee Park where the statue of Robert E. Lee was to be unveiled by President Roosevelt. The Packard was driven up beside the statue, which was completely covered, and a pull cord was handed to President Roosevelt, who was riding in the back seat. After a few words were spoken the cord was pulled and the covering dropped around the base of the statue.

Since I had previously visited the Century of Progress in Chicago in 1934, I was filled with civic pride over the grandeur of the Centennial Exposition in my own hometown. It was an exposition

President Franklin D. Roosevelt during his visit
to Dallas for the 1936 Texas Centennial

equal to a world's fair, except that it did not have pavilions of foreign countries.

All the major corporations had exhibits, including DuPont, General Electric, Sears and Roebuck, and Coca-Cola, as well as all the major oil companies and automakers.

The Hall of State was the centerpiece of the Exposition, and this magnificent building cost more per square foot to build than any building previously built in Texas. It contains an enormous great hall centered between two wings, each containing rooms dedicated to North, East, South, and West Texas, with murals in each depicting the characteristics of each section of Texas. The building was not fully completed in time for the opening of the Exposition, since the blue tile façade was not in place, and the large gold statue of a Native American was not yet hoisted over the entrance.

Some of the other Art Deco limestone buildings built for this occasion were the Museum of Natural History, the Museum of Fine Arts, now known as The Science Place, the Horticultural building, and the Aquarium, which at the time was the largest aquarium west of the Mississippi River.

Directly across the street from the Aquarium stands the Band Shell, where free nightly shows were presented. They featured all of the current comedian and vaudevillian entertainers of the day. One particular evening I recall when the very popular Amos and Andy were the featured performers, and I was fortunate enough to have them both autograph the brim of my jungle helmet, which I still have today.

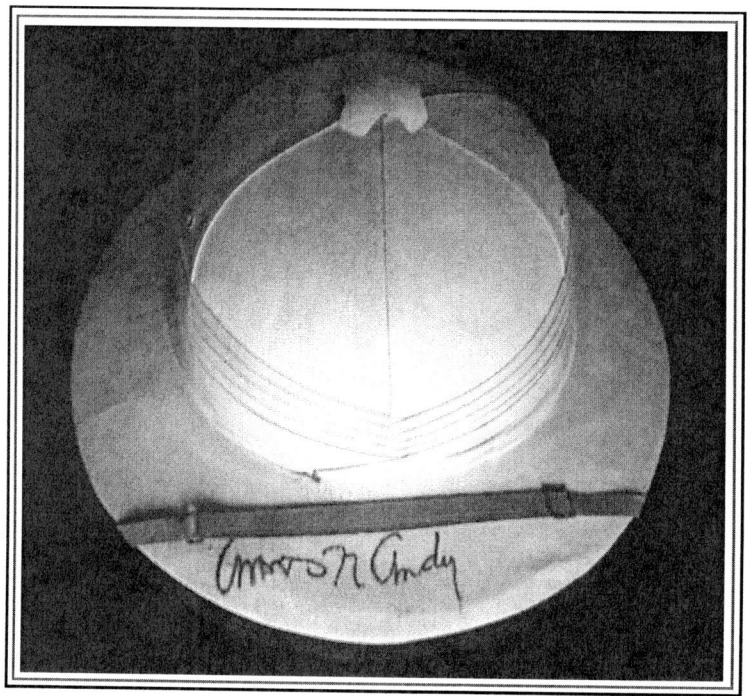

My pith helmet with Amos and Andy's autograph

Jungle helmets were very big probably due to the Frank Buck "Bring 'em Back Alive" movies of that era. Even the Centennial employees wore jungle helmets for identification.

General Motors leased what is now the Music Hall for the duration of the Exposition. Extensive remodeling was done to the interior to accommodate their pavilion. The first floor was built up to make it perfectly level from the stage to the back wall. It was made particularly strong as it had to support a display of new GM cars as well as the throngs who came to witness the stage show.

All during the summer of 1936 the big name bands of the era were brought to the GM stage on successive weeks, and they performed free of charge. The bands were highly publicized and their appearance boosted attendance to the Centennial.

In addition to the stage show, General Motors provided numerous technical and engineering displays in small rooms beneath the balcony, while on one side of the stage was a small theater where movies ran continually, showing the various aspects of automobile manufacturing. This building was totally air-conditioned, which added a great deal to its appeal.

Located on the space where the parking lot for the Music Hall now exists stood a replica of the English Globe Theater where Shakespearean plays were enacted. Also occupying a space in this same area was a federally constructed building known as the Hall of Negro Achievement. This was one of the many temporary structures built by the federal government for the Centennial.

A bit further down the street was the outdoor exhibit of the Sinclair Refining Company, which consisted of huge life-size models of dinosaurs to emphasize Sinclair's statement that crude oil was fifty million years in the making. They moved and made guttural noises.

Adjacent to the Sinclair exhibit was the Hall of Religion, which was devoted to various displays regarding the world's religions. A portion of this building remains today and is used as offices.

Directly next to the Hall of Religion on the corner of First Avenue and Grand, the Magnolia Petroleum Company built a very attractive Art Deco building known as the Magnolia Lounge. It contained a small theater where entertainment was provided. This is the first place that I ever heard a Hammond electric organ. The building also had a canopy-covered balcony, providing a shady place for people to sit and relax their tired feet.

Directly across First Avenue now stands the Old Mill Restaurant in a rustic building that originally housed a flour milling operation. The flour mill was actually two stories high within the building, and the second level had a balcony much like the mezzanine in a hotel. It completely surrounded the upper level of the flour mill. In front of the building was an operating water wheel, but it was not connected to any machinery. That is why the building is known today as the Old Mill.

Many people younger than me recall this building as the Borden Milk building, where Elsie the cow and her calf Beauregard were exhibited during subsequent state fairs in the '50s and '60s.

Next door to the Old Mill building the Gulf Radio studios were located in a temporary structure containing several sound studios with plate glass fronts. All day and evening, programs were broadcast throughout the Exposition grounds, with some of the entertainment being live, and some being recorded. One of the announcers was a very young Art Linkletter.

The many speakers located throughout the grounds were so acoustically designed that they totally blanketed the area with sound. As you walked out of the range of one speaker you entered the range of another.

Today Big Tex stands in a circle that was directly in front of the Gulf studios. Directly behind Big Tex now stands Grand Place, but during the Centennial this space was occupied by a huge temporary structure built by Ford Motor Company. Inside the building a semi-rotunda type area acted as a lobby, with multiple doors entering into the building proper. Above these doors was displayed various types of transportation, one of which was Henry Ford's original car. The safety people had been instructed that in the event of a fire to make sure that they remove Mr. Ford's car, even if nothing else was saved.

Inside the cavernous building various operations used in the manufacture of automobiles were displayed. There was also a small display room with many various models of perpetual motion type machines, none of which were functional on their own, but were actuated by a small electric motor. At the rear of the building was a large pavilion surrounded by tropical plants, and a stage on which Jose Manzanares and his South American orchestra performed daily.

To demonstrate the riding qualities of the new Fords, a road had been constructed around the lagoon, with the surface paved with various types of material. Sections of the road were built of cobblestones, concrete, asphalt, and there was even a section built of wooden timbers to replicate the old wooden highway from Yuma, Arizona to San Diego, California. People would line up to take their turn at a ride around the lagoon in one of the new Ford demonstration models to experience the ride.

Each night after dark, an impressive display of fireworks was presented.

One of my friends in the Early Ford V-8 club, Ernesto Castellon, currently owns the 1936 Ford phaeton that was actually used as one of the demonstrators during the Exposition. Ford also had a number of school buses, which made daily trips to the Ford assembly plant on East Grand Avenue. Visitors could board one of these buses to witness the assembly of 1936 cars and return to the grounds.

The building now known as the Tower Building was originally the Federal Building. The building was not temporary, since it was constructed of clay tile. Many expositions of the day used only temporary buildings, but it was determined that in those days a permanent building using clay tile could be built for about the same dollars as a temporary structure, and therefore many of the buildings in Fair Park today are survivors of the 1936 Texas Centennial.

The Federal Building had many interesting displays and dioramas. It even contained a printing press, where they demonstrated how money was printed. It was a most interesting and educational building.

After entering the front gate and completing a stroll of several hundred feet on tree-lined sidewalks, today you can witness the breathtaking beauty of the esplanade with identical buildings on either side, each reflecting in the water of the reflecting basin between them.

Six towering figures stand in arched openings and represent the six nations under whose flags Texas has stood. At night the area is illuminated like a fairyland. The building on the east side of the esplanade known as the Centennial Building was originally several buildings with streets between that were later joined together to form one building. The south end of this building, which was originally intended to be the Hall of Petroleum, was leased to the Chrysler Corporation due to delays on the part of the petroleum industry to negotiate the lease. Chrysler covered all of the walls with pale blue mirrors, air-conditioned the space, and displayed the 1936 cars in it. It also contained a theater where they staged marionette shows, as well as movies depicting how sturdy Chrysler cars were.

Most of the remaining display spaces in the Centennial Building were general exhibits by various corporations. Santa Fe Railroad had a very large, elaborate model train display, and the Southern Pine Association had an impressive display of various woods. The Petroleum industries' failure to negotiate the lease in time forced them to construct their own building, which was of a temporary nature and located in front of what is now the Food and Fiber Building near the Hall of State.

Across the esplanade from the Centennial Building on the west side of the reflecting basin was a building that had been created by incorporating the old Automobile Building with a portion of new construction running along the esplanade, forming a V-shaped building, since the original Automobile Building was directly parallel to First Avenue and would not fit the reflecting characteristics required for the three statues on that side of the esplanade.

This "V"-shaped building contained the exhibits of the DuPont Corporation, the General Electric House of Magic, the Coca-Cola exhibit, and the Sears & Roebuck Theater, which showed a film depicting fifty years of Sears & Roebuck.

Tragically, this entire structure was destroyed by fire

subsequent to World War II. The all-steel new automobile building was constructed at a later date on a line parallel with the reflecting basin. The matching towers and foyers accommodating the three statues were rebuilt in recent years. The reflecting basin today appears much as it did in 1936, thanks to the restoration.

With the exception of the limestone museum buildings, most of the display buildings were built of clay tile, which resulted in their lasting durability. The majority of the Exposition's buildings were of Art Deco design. Today they comprise the largest collection of Art Deco buildings in the world.

The midway was the focal point of the entertainment portion of the exposition. The major attractions were varied and colorful. They ranged from The Black Forest, a replica of a small German village that had an ice rink surrounded by tables and chairs where meals were served and ice shows were performed, to The Showboat, which had a façade of a Mississippi riverboat with a theater inside where the play "The Drunkard" was performed nightly. The audience was encouraged to cheer the hero, boo the villain, and clap for the heroine.

Directly across the street from The Showboat was the Streets of Paris, whose façade was the model of the prow of a modern ocean liner like the *Normandy*. Inside was built a replica of a Paris street, which featured girlie shows and souvenir shops. In the center of it all was a stage where cabaret shows were presented.

A little further up the street was Admiral Byrd's Little America, which was a re-creation of the structures erected at the South Pole for his expedition. A part of the exhibit was a Curtis Wright Condor aircraft, which had been used at the South Pole.

In order to gather a crowd for this presentation, they used a man who performed a mechanical man act. His actions were jerky and his face was expressionless and he never blinked his eyes, and it was not divulged that he was a human being until the end of the barker's spiel, at which time he broke his stance and spoke in an animated way about the exhibit inside. The show also included dog sleds, live huskies, and the fur clothing worn on the expedition.

Nearby was another burlesque show in the form of a slave

market, and they would bring out the girls in harem clothing to dance as an enticement to bring in the patrons. While I did get inside to see the Streets of Paris, I never penetrated the portals of the slave market since I was only 13 years old.

Robert L. Ripley had a huge building filled with unusual and strange items, including human beings that one would associate with a freak show.

Where the Livestock Coliseum now stands was a large grandstand, which had served the Fair Park Racetrack prior to the Centennial. It seated the patrons viewing the "Cavalcade of Texas," which depicted the history of Texas from the earliest days up to 1936. It was a grand production that was both educational and entertaining. There were Indians and cowboys and covered wagons, and Judge Roy Bean — "The Law West of the Pecos."

I was greatly saddened in the fall of 1936 to see the Centennial close; however, the following year, 1937, a follow-up exposition known as the Pan American Exposition, was staged at Fair Park. None of the major corporations were present, but I have heard that it was more profitable than the 1936 Centennial.

Chapter Ten

THE WAR YEARS

In the early '40s, insurance collectors were still a familiar sight in poor and middle class neighborhoods. People would take out a burial policy to insure having a proper burial, since most families had little cash reserve to meet such an expense. The policies were paid out in weekly installments.

Many people did not have checking accounts, and the weekly payment plans for many purchases were the norm. In those days many companies paid their employees in cash, and people dealt in cash.

It was during this time that a high-pressure salesman asked Al Smith if he could get a number of his friends together for a meeting. We met at the Smith's house not knowing what the purpose of the meeting was to be. The salesman was selling guitar lessons, which could be paid for on the aforementioned installment basis, and if you agreed to buy the lessons, they would give you a guitar.

He painted a rosy picture of how you could possibly pay for part of your college education with a band scholarship. Walter Hunt and Al Smith both fell for the pitch, but I felt that I could ill afford any monthly payments on anything as I didn't have any money to spare. I don't think either of the two boys ever mastered the guitar, but I'm sure there was some satisfaction in what they did learn.

After graduation from high school, the relationship between my mother and dad had become intolerable and he left home for the last time. He probably felt that I was now capable of picking up the slack financially as soon as I was employed and he would no longer be needed. On all previous reconciliations he had vowed to reform, but it never happened. So now I really was the man of the house. I never really envisioned going to college. Finding a job was my next challenge.

We used to buy refrigeration supplies from Beckett Electric Company, so I went there to apply for work. Percy Rollinson, who knew me, told me that I should apply at their Air-O-Line division, where they were making evaporative coolers and fluorescent light fixtures, which were to be installed in the new North American Aviation plant. They hired me immediately to work five days a week for the minimum wage of 30 cents an hour, or $12 a week, with absolutely no overtime.

I worked on the assembly line and in the warehouse. This job lasted about four months, until they completed the contract for the light fixtures and then everyone was laid off, so I was again in search of a job.

I read in the newspaper that North American Aviation Company was training men for employment at the new aviation plant they were building in Grand Prairie. They listed one of the jobs which involved tube bending, which is used in the production of aircraft. I applied and was accepted, but upon arrival at the building on Commerce Street where the training was to be done, I found that the tube bending equipment had already been shipped to the Grand Prairie plant and I was put into a class learning to do aircraft riveting.

We were paid a small wage while in training, and I used to drive my '34 Plymouth to work each day, and was able to park it without charge on Commerce Street.

There were no parking meters that far out on Commerce Street as yet. Parking meters were first introduced in downtown Dallas in 1934. This was a big event, and the pipes on which the meters were to be mounted were installed several weeks prior to the installation of the meters. After reading so much about the coming meters, some people thought that they should drop the nickel into the pipe. It was not a widespread practice, but was noted in the Dallas newspapers when some of the citizens committed this error.

Upon completion of the course in aircraft riveting, all students were dismissed and told that they would be contacted as soon as aircraft production was begun. Again I was searching for gainful employment to fill in until I heard from North American Aircraft.

The small side of the duplex where my mother and I still lived was vacated by the Gaines family when they bought a house, and Lola Patterson, the owner, remodeled and furnished it so her nephew Ernest Ray, and his new bride, Dorothy, could move in. Ernest was employed at Motor Parts Depot.

One day while I was talking to Ernest he told me that they were looking for a city deliveryman and that I should go down and put in my application with the store manager. I met with a Mr. Fred Small, and was immediately accepted at the princely sum of 32.5 cents per hour, with four hours a week at time and a half.

I started to work right away and had no problems, since I knew the city well. I had higher ambitions than being a city deliveryman, but Motor Parts had an aggressive advancement practice that started everyone as a deliveryman.

However, when someone left because of retirement or employment elsewhere, everybody moved up one step on the ladder. From deliveryman you went to the receiving department, from there to the shipping department, and from there to the counter, followed by becoming an outside salesman who called on the trade.

We had a machine shop that did machine work on automotive engines, as well as relining brakes and rebuilding clutch assemblies. This was specialized work, and therefore the personnel were more skilled and not involved in the standard advancement program. They also received better pay. It was usually necessary to hire a machinist if a vacancy occurred in the shop.

I enjoyed the job of deliveryman since we delivered far and wide throughout the city, which was considerably smaller than it is today. We valued our customers, and many times we delivered small items to far distant shops as an accommodation.

Hot shot, or non-scheduled deliveries, were prevalent, and

prior to WW II, were done by drugstores, parts houses, liquor stores, grocers, and other small businesses. Both gasoline and help were relatively inexpensive and it was used to cement customer relations.

On occasion, while delivering, I would find a license plate that someone had lost off their car. In those days you could call the County Clerk's office and obtain the name and address of the plate's owner. I would then notify them and they could pick up the plate at Motor Parts.

On one such occasion, I found a plate in the middle of Commerce Street in the area that is now known as Deep Ellum. When I called the owner's number, I was told that Mr. Baker was not in, and that I was speaking to his daughter, Barbara.

Recalling that I had been in a geometry class with a girl named Barbara Baker, I asked if she was one and the same. When she said yes, I recalled that she was a very attractive girl, and said I would, in this case, deliver the license plate to her home.

Several days passed and I received a call from Barbara stating that her father would like to have the plate. I took it over and renewed my acquaintance with her. A few days later the boys in our neighborhood decided we would like to have a picnic at White Rock Lake, and we all were to bring dates.

This seemed like a good opportunity for me to ask Barbara if she would like to go, and she accepted. It was at a place that the Corinthian Sailing Club is now located, and there were swings, a slide, and picnic tables. We must have had a good time because it turned out to be the beginning of a lengthy courtship, and after three and a half years we were married.

The marriage must have been a good one too, since it has lasted over 60 years. During my years as a member in the White Rock Rotary Club, one of the projects we decided to take on was trash cleanup around the lake, and during one of these cleanup days, we were photographed at the exact same spot where we had our picnic 60 years earlier. We felt at the time that we had truly come full circle since our first date.

White Rock Lake, where it all began 60 years earlier.

Now that I had steady employment, I felt that I could afford a better car than the '34 Plymouth, which was getting very tired. I answered a for sale ad in the paper for a 1937 Chrysler coupe, and the owner agreed to accept the Plymouth in trade. We struck a deal, and the Chrysler served me well throughout the war. The paint on it was poor, but it was mechanically sound and provided me with dependable transportation. After a new baby blue paint job, it was a very attractive little car. It was only four years old when I bought it, and I kept it until 1944 when I got out of the army.

When I wasn't delivering, I was expected to work inside the store for experience so that I might move up when and if the opportunity arose. Whenever possible, I would work in the machine shop, since I had had experience overhauling the Model T and the '34 Plymouth, as well as general mechanical aptitude.

Their machinist was an older man named Mr. Schlief. He was

My 1937 Chrysler

more than glad to teach me the auto machinist trade, and I was an eager student. When Mr. Schlief's subordinate machinist left for greener pastures, the company was desperate to find a replacement. Machinists were in short supply since most of them were going to work for the defense industry. Mr. Schlief told the management that I was capable of doing the job, and that they should make me an automotive machinist. That was the start of my career in the machine shop.

During my first days in the machine shop, business was rather slow, the reason being that prior to WW II, when cars got old and needed extensive engine overhauls or rebuilding, they were usually sold for scrap.

At that time, it was a rare occasion to get out the boring bar or machine and bore cylinder blocks out to an oversize, and most of my time was spent relining brake shoes and clutch plates, learning to read micrometers, and learning to operate the various machines in the shop. I enjoyed the work very much, as it afforded different challenges each day.

This was 1941 and we were not as yet engaged in WW II. Some of the fellows were getting drafted. But since they were not taking draftees or volunteers under the age of 21 unless they had the consent of their parents or dependents, I was not subject to military service at this time.

There was a tire store immediately next door to Motor Parts Depot, and one day the manager came over and talked to Mr. Peterman, who was our top operations manager. He told him quite confidentially that he thought Mr. Peterman should buy a new set of tires for his car. Mr. Peterman took the suggestion to heart, had a new set of tires put on his car, and within a few days all tire sales were frozen and tires were available only for essential vehicles such as police cars, fire trucks, etc. It was being realized that rubber from Southeast Asia was apt to become non-existent due to the embargoes we had put on Japan.

Three or four of the young men in the organization were members of a cavalry unit of the National Guard and were soon mobilized. On Sunday, December 7, 1941, my mother and I were just finishing our noon meal when my neighborhood friend, Al Smith, came to our house to tell us that the Japanese were bombing Pearl Harbor.

It would be pretty safe to say that most Americans did not even know where Pearl Harbor was, but we all soon found out. The next day, December 8, was my birthday. Our involvement in the war would have profound effects on everyone. An air of uncertainty and anxiety prevailed. The government immediately put into effect a program of rationing and priorities for the purchase of war essential materials. Detroit was allowed to continue making cars until February, at which time all auto production ceased and plants were converted to the construction of war materials.

I continued working in the machine shop as business increased dramatically. With no new cars available, people realized that they had to make their vehicles last for the duration of the war, and consequently did not hesitate to do engine overhauls or rebuilds as the case required.

Mr. Schlief left to work in the defense industry, and the company hired a young man by the name of Milton Pokladnik to work in the shop with me. The auto repair shops in town began doing a flourishing business, and our services were much in demand. A garage would disassemble an auto engine and call us to come out and measure the amount of wear with our micrometers, and inform them as to the extent of wear and remedies required to put the engine back in a serviceable condition. If the wear was not too excessive on the cylinders and the crank shaft bearing surfaces, we would take the pistons and connecting rods into the shop and fit new piston pins, piston rings, and engine bearings before returning them to the garage for reassembly. Badly worn cylinders and crank shafts called for a total rebuild, in which case the engine was removed and sent to our shop to be bored out to an oversize.

With many mechanics in the service, as well as many working in the defense plants, getting one's auto repaired became quite a challenge. Milton and I were frequently asked to work on people's cars on weekends, and this became a desirable source of additional income. After working all day, we would tear down an engine in our backyard on Friday night, take the parts to be machined to work Saturday morning, and reassemble the engine after work on Saturday afternoon.

We did good work at reasonable prices considering that we would overhaul a Ford or Chevrolet for $50 plus parts. We had many satisfied customers. We earned the reputation of being pretty good shade tree mechanics.

As the war intensified, civilian items virtually disappeared from the marketplace. Everything was scarce. There were no new refrigerators or kitchen appliances of any kind, including metal pots and pans.

We had regular scrap drives when all things made of metal were collected for recycling into war material. They even conducted scrap rubber drives, but recycled rubber was never very satisfactory, and a big push to develop synthetic rubber was introduced. A few tires were constructed of recycled rubber, but they were not very dependable, and still required a permit from the Office of Price Administration for their purchase. A price of one cent a pound was paid for scrap rubber, and the Dallas paper carried a story about some enterprising youngsters who had come into possession of some lead, probably obtained through illegal means, which they heated and tediously poured into an old garden hose so it would weigh more. They did not realize that lead had a far greater scrap value than rubber.

The Mercantile Bank building was built in the early '40s during World War II and its construction was made possible during the war years because the government needed additional office space in Dallas. All construction during the war had to have specific priorities in order to obtain building materials and equipment. One of our neighbors, Mr. J. G. Roney, who was with T&P Railroad, designated it the "Jap" building. During the war it was not politically incorrect to refer to the Japanese as Japs.

As a matter of fact, with the severe shortage of rubber, people were asked to turn in the rubber floor mats from the driver's compartment of their cars. If you complied with this request you were given a sticker to go in the back window of your car that read, "I gave my mat to slap a Jap."

I doubt that any of the rubber mats or old tires donated were ever used for the war effort, but everybody was very patriotic and wanted to do anything they could to help.

As time went on, more and more things were rationed, and ultimately you had to obtain a coupon to buy a new pair of shoes, and everyone was allowed only two coupons a year.

We were issued ration coupons for the purchase of meat and sugar, and housewives were encouraged to sell their accumulated grease and fats back to the meat market where it was collected and used in the production of ammunition.

Soap was very scarce, too, and my mother used her grease and a can of lye to make homemade laundry soap. She and Barbara put their old perfumes in it to make it smell better.

It became necessary to turn in your old toothpaste tube in order to buy a new tube of toothpaste, since the tubes at that time were made mostly out of zinc. Most grocers maintained a stash of scarce items such as black pepper, which they supplied to their regular customers.

Nylon stockings were out of production, and women resorted to every way imaginable to keep what pairs they had in use. At the Grand Silver ten-cent store on the ground floor of the Wilson Building was a little counter where several ladies sat with little gadgets that were used to re-weave runs in nylon stockings. It was a very busy place and never in need of customers.

Pleats in the fronts of men's pants, as well as cuffs, were eliminated in order to conserve material. People were very conservative in protecting their clothes, and should a tear appear in a garment, they could be repaired by a process known as in-weaving. This was accomplished by removing a small piece from the hem of the garment, fraying the edges and in-weaving it into the damaged portion of the tear.

Gasoline was also rationed, and the basic allotment allowed for three gallons a week for persons having an "A" sticker on their windshield. Provisions for more gasoline were allowed by the OPA for essential driving such as emergency vehicles, defense workers who traveled to and from their jobs, doctors, and any others driving excessive miles due to the war effort.

Gas rationing was initially instituted to conserve rubber, but with no limitations for boats or off-road vehicles. However, this stance changed due to the large amount used by the Air Force and the military, and soon it was rationed for all purposes. A national speed limit of 35 miles per hour was enforced, which made highway travel slow and tedious. This law was widely disobeyed.

Love Field, which had been our civilian airport for many years, was expanded and commissioned as an army airfield that would serve both commercial and military aircraft for the duration. While I was still below the then current military draft age of 21, and could have been deferred from military service due to my employment in an essential industry keeping the trucks, buses and automobiles running, as well as the fact that my mother was dependent on me for her support, I probably would never had been drafted into service. But, as most of my friends were either being drafted or volunteering for service, I felt it was my duty to do my part to contribute to the war effort.

I drove out to Love Field, since I knew they had been accepting volunteers for initial service and training at that base. I only got as far as the guard on the gate, who told me they were not accepting any more volunteers at that time.

Shortly thereafter, a large advertisement ran in the Dallas papers that stated that if you volunteered for the Army Air Force, you could choose any of several air bases in Texas for your basic training. Two fellow workers, Vernon Lyles and George Patterson, and I decided that we would enlist in the Army Air Force.

I figured that an army payroll allotment to my mother would amount to almost as much as I was contributing from my meager paycheck. So I went down to the enrollment office to sign up for service at one of the Texas air bases.

Love Field was not included on the list of available assignments. When I entered the office, I encountered one of my cousins, Ann Hill, working as a secretary. She asked me what I was doing there, and I told her I was there to enlist. She took me to an outer office and introduced me to an enlistment sergeant, Sgt. McDevitt, who was to fill out the enlistment papers.

He asked me where I was requesting assignment and I told him I had tried to enlist at Love Field but had been told they were not accepting any more volunteers. He then opened one of his lower desk drawers and removed a blank, signed request form from the commanding officer at Love Field.

He told me that they were furnished to him for his discretionary use in recruiting promising young men who he thought would make good airmen. The document was attached to my enlistment papers and was sent with me to the reception center at Mineral Wells, Texas. It requested that following my induction that I was to be assigned to Love Field in Dallas.

Prior to my induction physical examination, I had to go to the Texas Employment Commission for a mental examination, which consisted of no more than asking me a few basic questions about my name, my age, and my address, none of which would constitute a mental examination.

But as of October 1942, the country was badly in need of military personnel, and volunteers made it a quicker process than the draft. When I took my physical, there was a man in front of me who had only one eye, and I felt sure that he would be a reject. But to my astonishment, I encountered him at Mineral Wells dressed in his new military uniform.

Barbara and I had been going together for about a year, and although I elected not to sell my car when I went into the service, I didn't want to set it up on blocks as many service men did. Barbara had agreed to drive it occasionally since my mother did not know how to drive.

Barbara and my dad went with me to the U.S. Post Office and courthouse located on Bryan Street in downtown Dallas. There I was sworn in, and I still recall the feeling of anxiety and uncertainty that I felt when I raised my hand and pledged to defend the country and the constitution for the duration of the war, plus six months.

No one knew how long the war would last, and it was going very badly for the Allies at that time. The newly enlisted group boarded a Greyhound bus with nothing but the clothes on our backs and a shaving kit. We departed for Camp Walters, located in Mineral Wells, Texas, and arrived there, driving at the 35-mile-an-hour speed, in about three hours.

It was there that I received my initial immunization shots, and was issued a complete uniform, including a heavy overcoat. The out-of-season clothing was carried in two barracks bags.

While I was satisfied that my request for assignment to Love Field was attached to my paperwork, I was very apprehensive whether or not the assignment would take place. Those of us who were expecting to be assigned to Dallas had been told initially that we would first go to Las Vegas, New Mexico for our basic training.

The third day we were assembled and walked to the railhead,

where we boarded a train for departure. As we left Mineral Wells, a man in our group who had been a railroad man said we had passed the switch that would have directed us west toward New Mexico. He didn't know where we were going, but we were not on the track to Las Vegas.

When we reached the Texas and Pacific station in Fort Worth, it was quite evident that we were going either to or through Dallas to reach our destination. About an hour later we arrived at the Dallas Union Station and were instructed to take our bags and disembark from the train. A soldier met us and told us to wait in front of the station and we would be picked up. After a lengthy wait, a bus showed up and loaded us up and took us out to Love Field.

Much of the military barracks and facilities were under construction, and as it turned out, the officer of the day did not know we were coming and had no idea what to do with us.

We were told that the next day we were to re-activate an abandoned Civilian Conservation Corps camp on the shores of White Rock Lake. But this could not be accomplished until it was daylight. This presented quite a problem for the officer in charge of us, until one of the men told him that most of us were from Dallas and could go home that night. A couple of guys piped up and said they weren't from Dallas, so where were they supposed to go, and they immediately received many invitations to spend the night with some of the locals.

The lieutenant then decided that he would order a two-and-a-half-ton truck from the motor pool, which operated 24 hours a day, and send us downtown with instructions not to get caught by the military police, since none of us had a pass and none were available.

They let us off on Pacific Street and everybody scattered. I had a little money in my pocket and soon located a pay telephone and called Barbara and asked her if she would like to see me tonight. She couldn't believe this was possible until I told her where I was.

She agreed to pick me up and took me to my mother's house, where she already had a little flag with a blue star hanging in the front window indicating that someone in that house was in the service. She, too, was surprised to see me.

We visited until Barbara went home. The next morning I drove my car out to Love Field, thinking I would be allowed to drive myself out to Camp White Rock. This was not to be, and we were all loaded into trucks and taken to the camp.

I was quite concerned about my car being left on the street and not knowing when I would be able to retrieve it. We filed into an empty barracks and received a folding cot. The old barracks were really primitive and were heated with a large pot-bellied coal stove.

I calculated where the best place would be to put my cot in relation to the stove. I sat it up just far enough away from the stove that I thought it would be comfortable, but near enough to stay warm. Since we were the first group into the barracks, we had some liberty as to where we wanted our cots lined up.

It was rather cool, since it was mid-October, and the stove provided a welcome source of warmth. This arrangement worked out very well until the middle of the first night when a sergeant came in and said they had a new group of recruits, and that we should all put our cots closer together toward the back of the barracks. This move resulted in my cot being immediately in front of the door by the stove. The outcome was that often when the stove was stoked, coal was dropped into my bed. This happened several times each night.

On the first morning after breakfast in the makeshift mess hall, we were assembled on the drill field. A staff sergeant addressed us and asked how many had had ROTC in high school. There was only a few, and of course I raised my hand, and we were told that we would become drill instructors to teach the recruits basic training and close order drill. We were made acting sergeants.

This relieved us from KP duty, since we were more urgently needed to teach the trainees rather than to peel potatoes and wash dishes.

I was still quite concerned about my car, and told the staff sergeant in charge of my problem. He went to the commanding officer of the camp and obtained a pass for me. I got a ride back to Love Field on one of the supply trucks and was able to retrieve my car and take it home. Barbara took me back to camp after she got off from work that afternoon.

A second series of shots were administered while we were at White Rock. Vernon Lyles, who had been a co-worker of mine at Motor Parts, was directly in front of me in the line to receive our shots. As the line moved forward, he was watching everyone else as they were stuck in the arm. It must have had quite an effect on him, since when he stepped up to get his shot he passed out cold. After he was revived, we teased him greatly about this incident.

After about two weeks at Camp White Rock I received orders to report to Love Field. Classification had reviewed my file as to my civilian experience and decided that I should be assigned to the motor pool.

The air base at Love Field was still under construction and everything was extremely disorganized. I was originally assigned as a staff car driver until the vehicle repair shop was completed, at which time I was assigned to the parts room. It was my responsibility to requisition needed parts and supplies for the maintenance of the jeeps, trucks, and automobiles used on the base. This was one example where the army correctly utilized the civilian experience of a serviceman.

In addition to running the parts room, I was also dispatched on special orders to numerous other military bases to either deliver or pick up military vehicles. Under the ruling of capabilities, our shop was considered to be a second-echelon shop, which meant that we could change oil and tires and do minor repairs and maintenance. But we had many men who could do more extensive repairs.

This was the result of the recruiting program for high-quality personnel on our base. If the necessary parts were available, we could perform engine overhauls and do clutch, brake, and transmission work. If the needed parts for these jobs were not available to us, I had many connections with automotive jobbers and parts houses in the Dallas area and was able to trade to them items such as spark plugs, fuel pumps, etc. for parts we needed such as piston rings, wheel bearings, and clutch assemblies.

This allowed us to put the vehicles back into service with little delay. We were required to report daily the number of vehicles that were inoperable.

I was also required to occasionally stand guard on the flight line during the night to protect the aircraft parked there. One night a windstorm developed and some of the planes on which the pilots had failed to set the parking brakes blew all over the field. We called for help and some of the crew chiefs came out and set the brakes. The next morning the pilots had to line them up in proper order.

On another occasion, the crew operating the fuel truck had too much to drink and crashed it into one of the planes. These guys were court-martialed for dereliction of duty and served time in the guardhouse.

We had a number of fatal crashes, both on the field and off. Since most of the time I was on duty in the parts room, I was available for, and assigned to, emergency crash investigations and drove the crash investigator and photographer to the scene of the accident.

We had a contingent of Women's Army Service Pilots (WASPs) stationed at the field. One evening while approaching the field in a P-47 Thunderbolt, the woman pilot clipped a power pole on the east side of the field and knocked out all of the lights on and around Love Field. She maintained control of the plane, pulled up, and began circling the field. Without lights she could not attempt to land.

A frantic call to the motor pool requested that we rush any and all vehicles with headlights to a seldom used east/west runway. We lined up jeeps, trucks, and passenger cars on either side of the runway and awaited her final approach. It was just after dusk and we could see the plane as it came in.

On her initial attempts she undershot the field and dropped completely out of our sight behind a knoll. Each time she did this we assumed that she had crashed, but with the sound of the huge engine revving up in the P-47, we were reassured that she was still in the air. She would just top the crest of the knoll. But on her first few passes she was not lined up with the runway. Ground personnel had already seen that she had knocked off the flaps on one side of the plane, and had instructed her not to apply any flaps when she landed. This meant that the P-47, which was a very hot airplane, would have to land very fast.

On about her third attempt she touched down and used the entire runway before getting the plane stopped. She stepped out of the cockpit unhurt, but the entire bottom of the plane had been torn away.

This lady still visits the Flight Museum, and I have seen her interviewed recently on television recalling this incident. A couple of years ago Barbara and I attended a program at the Flight Museum at Love Field, and heard that this same lady was to be on the program. I took some pictures I had of the motor pool personnel, and after the program I introduced myself and showed her the pictures of the guys who had guided her in on that fateful night.

She was most appreciative and excited to talk to someone who had actually been there. I told her she had related the event just exactly the way I remembered it.

My most harrowing experience involved an accident that occurred in the repair shop. A soldier changing a fuel line on a vehicle we called a Dodge carryall, which would be considered an SUV today, was seriously burned. While he was removing the line, some fuel ran down his arm and was ignited by a spark from a welder at the other end of the shop.

When he was pulled from underneath the truck, he was completely engulfed in flames, and a number of men worked feverishly to extinguish the fire. The fuel line was still loose, the tank was full and gasoline continued to run out and feed the flames beneath the truck.

Every army vehicle had a fire extinguisher as equipment. It was filled with carbon tetrachloride, which when vaporized blocks the oxygen from around the flame. Another sergeant and I began emptying fire extinguishers on the flame under the truck. At first, it washed most of the gasoline and fire out from under the truck and against the back wall of the building where the flames raced up the wall without igniting the structure.

We continued grabbing extinguishers from other vehicles in the shop, emptying them on the fire that was still being fed by draining gasoline. We were never successful in completely putting the fire out until a fire truck appeared with a carbon dioxide extinguisher. The fumes from the carbon tetrachloride are very poisonous and my lungs were damaged and caused a great deal of pain. The soldier who was burned spent several months in the Ashburn General Hospital in McKinney, Texas. This particular type of extinguisher fluid is has now been outlawed for use in fire extinguishers.

Aside from being a chemical that was effective in fire fighting, carbon tetrachloride was also used as a dry cleaning solvent. Several years ago, a well-known Dallas theater celebrity named Margo Jones died as a result of this chemical having been used to clean the carpets in her apartment.

Shortly after the fire I was ordered to take a convoy of vehicles to an air base in Midland, Texas and return by train to Dallas. Upon my return, I experienced severe breathing difficulties and reported to the infirmary thinking I probably had pneumonia since my chest was tight.

The doctor who looked at me said, "You don't have pneumonia, you have asthma." He administered a shot of adrenaline, which gave me almost immediate relief. He then ordered me to report to Ashburn General Hospital for allergy tests.

I had not experienced an asthma attack since I was in Junior High school and had assumed that I had outgrown the disease. I have always felt that its reoccurrence was the result of inhaling too much carbon tetrachloride during that fire. I had not even disclosed that I had been asthmatic at the time I enlisted.

Unfortunately, I have never been free of it again and carry an inhaler at all times. After several weeks in the hospital and undergoing numerous allergy tests, it was found that I was allergic to many contaminants and inhalants, and I was sent back to Love Field classified as "Limited Duty – Unfit for Overseas Service."

After returning to Love Field I resumed my customary duties until I experienced another severe asthma attack for which I reported on sick call to get a shot of adrenaline. Much to my surprise I was returned to Ashburn General Hospital, where I was honorably discharged on June 15, 1944.

D Day, or the invasion of Europe, had occurred just a week

Me in my Staff Sergeant's uniform

before and I always felt that the Defense Department thought this signaled the beginning of the end of hostilities in Europe, and hastened the discharge of all limited service personnel. After the successful landing on Normandy and the rapid early progress of the Allies into enemy territory, severe fighting such as the Battle of the Bulge was not anticipated.

Even though the war in Europe was closer to victory than it was in the South Pacific where island-hopping battles raged on, no one knew how long it was going to take to defeat Japan.

While I was in the hospital there were many servicemen who had served on Guadalcanal and had been returned to the states after contracting asthma in the jungles of the South Pacific. They had never had it before and no one knew what had caused them to contract it.

The end of the war in 1945 was a most welcome time, and while we knew it would take a few years for things to get back to normal again, knowing it was over was a great relief.

It was a great feeling driving out on the runway to meet the pilots coming back to Love Field on their final flights, and since many of the ferry pilots that flew cargo and troops here in the states were women, many of them were sent to Love Field to turn in their planes as well.

I had the honor of picking up two of these brave women on their last flight in, and we marked the side of the plane with chalk to commemorate the last flight, day, and time.

Shuttling two lady ferry pilots from their plane
after their final mission at the end of WW II.

I was now ready to resume a civilian occupation and to start earning some of the increase in wages that had been enjoyed by the civilian workforce while I was in service. My pre-war employer learned of my discharge and wanted me to return as one of their machinists as soon as possible. It took a bit of negotiation, since they wanted to hire me back at nearly the same rate as I was making before the war. I told them that this was less than I was being paid as a Staff Sergeant in the Army, where I didn't have to buy my own clothes.

We finally agreed on an hourly wage that was acceptable to me, and with practically no time off, I started back to work.

Barbara was working for the Dept. of Agriculture in offices at the Wilson Building, and we decided to set a date for our wedding. We became engaged at Christmas in 1943. We decided to wait until the end of the war in order for me to accumulate some money. I was still driving the Chrysler coupe, but wished to get a later model, since it was eight years old and had quite high mileage.

Chapter Eleven

THE POSTWAR YEARS

I had always admired convertibles and had a great desire to own one. Barbara and I started shopping around, we looked at Fords, Chevrolets, and Plymouths, all of which we felt were too war weary.

An ad in the Dallas paper advertised a 1939 Buick Century convertible, and we decided to go and take a look. Upon examination, we found the car to be in very nice condition and quite low mileage. It was black and had a tan top and red interior. Most important of all, it had side mounted spare tires in the front fenders and was a most impressive car.

The negatives were that the white sidewall tires were about two-thirds worn down, and the treads had been regrooved with a grooving iron, which was the practice in those days, but is now illegal. Also, the engine was not firing on two of its eight cylinders.

The current owner, a lady nurse, was told that it needed a valve grinding job, and this no doubt was why she was selling the car. We made a deal to buy the car as is, and Barbara's father loaned me $1,000, to which I added about $150, in order to buy it.

My Chrysler coupe was paid for, and I sold it almost immediately for $650, which I turned over to Barbara's dad, and with money earned doing after-hours mechanical work, I was able to pay him off before Christmas and our impending wedding.

Upon close examination and diagnosis, I discovered that the Buick had a faulty vacuum pump, which was causing the engine malfunction and was easily corrected by installing a rebuilt pump. Barbara and I really felt like SOMEBODY when driving around in such a gorgeous car.

It was a great performer since it had the biggest engine that Buick made at that time, and would be today a very desirable and expensive collector car. Unfortunately, I wasn't able to keep all of the cars I fell in love with over the years, and all we have to remind us of that great little Buick is a picture on the wall.

Our 1939 Buick Century convertible

It was very difficult in those days to hire machinists as they were in great demand at the aircraft plants. Milton Pokladnik and I worked a lot of the time without additional assistance in the machine shop at Motor Parts Depot. We occasionally were able to have a third man who could help with cleanup and non-precision type work.

We put in lots of overtime, but generally did an engine overhaul for someone on weekends, since we only worked half a day on Saturday. This was done in the Lindsley Avenue backyard on a concrete driveway.

In addition to the above endeavors, I also became active in buying and selling used cars. I would buy one and service it and do needed mechanical repairs, and offer it for sale with an ad in the local paper. The war was just winding down and new cars were not yet in production, so good serviceable used cars were easily sold.

We set our wedding date for New Years Eve 1944, and during those war years weddings were much less complicated than they are today. We were married in Barbara's family church, Mount Auburn Christian, at 4:00 P.M. Sunday afternoon, with a small reception following at her parent's house. Several years later due to the dwindling congregation, the church was disbanded and the building sold to the Hare Krishna sect. We get a kick out of telling people we were married in the Hare Krishna Temple.

Barbara and me in 1944

We had rented a small duplex on Worth Street, which was very minimal in that it was a one family conversion and didn't have a normal bedroom, but had a canvas-enclosed screened porch. It was very little comfort on a cold January night, but we had our love to keep us warm. Apartments were almost non-existent during the war years, since there had been virtually no new construction since 1941 due to building material shortages. Many homeowners had converted their houses into multiple apartments to take advantage of the opportunity. Some of these conversions were pretty bad, but anything with a roof that would house a family was readily rented.

One apartment we looked at required that you go through the bathroom to access the kitchen. We passed on that one.

On January 1, we departed for our honeymoon in San Antonio. That was as far as we could go on the gas coupons we had. My grandfather, who had been in the hotel business for many years, was a personal friend of Artie Compton, the manager of the Gunter Hotel in San Antonio. He had written Artie, telling him of our plans to stay there on our honeymoon, and he assigned us the bridal suite, which was a great improvement over the canvas-covered sleeping quarters we had occupied the night before.

Upon returning to Dallas, we went back to the duplex where we stayed for about two weeks. Jimmy Shevlin, an army buddy of mine who lived with his wife, Jessie, in the other side of the duplex where my mother lived, told me that he had been put on detached service to India. He would be leaving soon and hated to leave his wife alone.

After a brief discussion, it was decided that she would move in with my mother and we could move into their side while he was gone. Fortunately it was furnished, as we didn't own a stick of furniture. We jumped at the opportunity to make the move, and it worked out real well with Jessie and my mother sharing her side of the duplex. Jimmy was gone about two years, and during that time we enjoyed having our own place.

In a few months the war ended and Jimmy returned to Dallas and wanted his apartment back. Barbara and I gave up the apartment and moved into the large side of the duplex where we occupied the upper floor, while my mother retained the downstairs.

We shared a kitchen and bath and slept on a mattress on the floor, since we still didn't have any furniture. There was no heat up there, and it was almost as cold as the apartment with the canvas porch. As good fortune would have it, electric blankets were introduced about then and it solved our problem.

Barbara continued to work for the Dept. of Agriculture, and my job afforded me a good deal of overtime, so with these two salaries, plus my shade tree overhauls and used car dealing, we were feeling pretty prosperous.

Immediately after the war, new cars were very difficult to come by. But through my friendship with Stuart Campbell, whose father was a Ford dealer in Forney, Texas, I was able to get a new 1946 Ford Club Coupe at the ceiling price, which was controlled by the Office of Price Administration. We were quite thrilled to be able to buy a new Ford for $1,208.72.

From the time I was in high school I had the desire to attend the Indianapolis 500 Mile auto race, which is held on Memorial Day each year. A friend of mine, George Goodwin, had also wanted to see the race one day. Together we decided that Barbara, George, and I would drive up in the new Ford to satisfy this long held ambition.

It was the first of many trips to Indy we made in subsequent years. I would like to be able to say the Ford was a good car, but it shed nuts and bolts like a wet dog sheds water and leaked like a sieve every time it rained.

In the course of my sales job I traveled all over the city of Dallas and made many friends throughout the city. This allowed me a lot of opportunities to buy used cars and fix them up for resale. Sometimes I bought them in partnership with others, but most of the time it was a personal enterprise. After buying, I would bring them home to do mechanical repairs, clean the interiors, and wash and polish the exteriors. Sometimes I even had them repainted if they needed it. Then they were ready for resale.

I always had willing customers, as people knew I knew good cars when I saw them, and I conducted this backyard endeavor for many years. This enabled us to acquire a few things that we would not otherwise have been able to afford. As production resumed on civilian products, we, like other newlyweds, needed everything and this source of additional income was most welcome.

One Sunday afternoon while I was in the backyard doing my thing with a car, my mother and Barbara were cooking lunch and decided they would have some drinks. We had bought some prepackaged mix for Manhattans and they mixed up a little batch, tasted it, and decided it needed something else.

They kept mixing and tasting, mixing and tasting, until when I finally came in to eat they both were sitting at the table giggling and half crocked. Barbara couldn't even hit her mouth with a fork of food. To quote the great comedy team of Laurel and Hardy, "It was a fine how-do-you-do."

Dallas, up until after World War II, was a "dry" city, meaning that no one could buy a mixed drink at a restaurant, bar, or eating place, other than a bottle of beer. Package stores carried premixed cocktails you could take home for your own consumption as well as hard liquors by the bottle, but there was no on-site consumption.

Most people were quite unsophisticated in the realm of mixed drinks and cocktails and it was a new experience for my mother and my wife.

Actually, the acceptance of mixed drinks was a step towards making Dallas a more cosmopolitan city, but there are still pockets in Dallas that have remained "dry" due to a local option law that was invoked by some of the more religious groups who did not want liquor stores in their neighborhoods in the early years.

During the years of Prohibition, while liquor was outlawed, people became very industrious in their endeavors toward finding a drink when they wanted one. Some of the die-hard alcoholics even resorted to drinking common household chemicals that contained alcohol. Some of the more common ones were mouthwash and shaving lotions. Bay Rum aftershave was a very popular alternative at the time.

Private stills began to spring up all around Dallas. I was aware of one back in the woods just off the intersection of Lakeland Drive and Garland Road. When the wind was coming from the right direction you could smell it as you drove down Garland Road.

Bathtub gin was a very common form of homemade liquor during the day. An interesting side-note to the duplex we lived in on Lindsley Avenue was that during Prohibition some bootleggers had lived there and erected a still in a room on the second floor for distilling their homemade whiskey. This we know to be true because there is a burned circle in the hardwood floor where the still was located.

My dad and his brother probably knew some of the bootleggers of the day, since my dad was a friend of Benny Binyon, one of the most notorious of Dallas' early day gamblers and bootleggers.

Supposedly there was a tunnel dug from under the kitchen floor to the detached garage in the back yard that would allow the bootleggers to transport their goods from the house to their car without being detected. The trap door in the kitchen floor was still present at the time we lived there and Dad and Harry tried several times to find the tunnel, but were never successful in finding any sign of it.

The tenant that lived there before us was a school teacher at J. L. Long Jr. High School, and upon moving in found several one gallon jugs of moonshine in the attic.

Several years after we had moved away and built our own home, the owner did a major renovation to the duplex to get it fixed up and ready for sale. We went through it to see what he had done to improve on it since the days we were tenants, and much to our surprise the burned spot on the floor was still in the upstairs room. The owner didn't know how it got there, but he didn't try to remove it, and was really surprised when I told him the story.

After hearing it, he decided he was glad he left it there and thought the unusual folklore added some color to the history of the old house.

While on the surface it may seem like these were difficult times, actually they were great days. We were newly married, had a Chris Craft speedboat on White Rock Lake, a new car, and were living in a furnished duplex.

It was about this time that we began to start accumulating

our own furniture, and we bought our first bedroom suite with a mahogany four-poster bed, a mahogany cedar chest, which was a Christmas present to Barbara, and a Magnavox radio-phonograph.

Strange as it may seem, housewives were usually pretty thrilled to receive appliances and household items, which had been unavailable since 1941. Meletio Electric Company was located about 75 feet from the back door of Motor Parts Depot. The salespeople there would let us know when they received a shipment of waffle irons, toasters, blenders, coffee makers, etc., and I was one that never let one of those opportunities pass me by.

My mother and I had had several black cats over the years, and we had one named Blackie when Barbara and I married. The breakfast room on Lindsley had a loose screen on the window and Blackie had learned how to push it out when he wanted out and pull it open when he wanted in.

One day Blackie disappeared. We looked everywhere, and even advertised in the paper for him, but no luck. We finally gave up and ended up getting another black cat that we named Cinder.

About six weeks later we were awakened in the middle of the night by the darnedest cat fight you ever heard. We got up, turned on the light, and saw two black cats really going at it. Blackie had come home. He was in real good condition and we felt like he had been taken by someone and just managed to escape. The two cats finally got along peacefully, but didn't really like one another.

All during the war years rents were controlled by the Office of Price Administration to curb inflation. My mother had rented the Lindsley Avenue duplex for many years prior to rent control and was paying $25 a month plus utilities.

After Barbara and I moved in, we voluntarily raised the rent to $50 where it remained until rent controls were removed in 1948. Almost immediately the owner raised the rent to $100, and we decided it was time for us to find a home of our own.

We had saved in excess of $5,000 for the purpose of eventually buying a house. We began looking at pre-owned homes in the East Dallas area, but didn't find one with the required amenities to suit our needs. We thought we should have at least three bedrooms,

Barbara and Blackie – 1946

since my mother would be living with us for a while.

A young couple was living in the other side of the duplex and I happened to mention to him that we had looked at a new house just off Buckner Blvd. in the new Lake Highlands addition. He then told me that he was a home builder and had several lots available just off of Garland Road in the Casa Linda addition.

We decided to let him build us a house on one of the lots, and he had his brother, who was also a builder, draw up a plan to our specifications. As well as the needed bedroom space, we also wanted a separate dining room, a wood-burning fireplace, and a two-car garage. We approved the plans and the price, which was $14,000.

Neither of our parents had ever owned their own homes, and we felt very fortunate to have the ability to buy our ranch style house.

– 129 –

I obtained a V.A. loan for $8,500 at the rate of 4%. This low rate was obtained through the G.I. Bill of Rights, enacted for the benefit of the veterans of World War II. Barbara was still working for the U.S. Department of Agriculture, so we elected to pay an extra $100 per month, enabling us to retire the loan after only seven years. The foundation was laid out on the first day of June 1948. Our new address would be 9223 San Fernando Way.

For the first few years following WW II, life in the U.S. was much the same as it was prior to the attack on Pearl Harbor in 1941. New homes and cars had changed very little from the pre-war years.

Only very expensive homes were equipped with central heat at that time, so our house had a combination of space heaters in the bedrooms and bath, and a floor furnace in the living room. There was nothing like standing over the floor furnace after coming in from the cold, even if all of our shoes ended up with a waffle pattern on the bottoms.

There were also folding wooden racks that could be bought for hanging wet laundry. We used one over the floor furnace to dry diapers and towels.

Once appliances became available, we were among the first on the block to have a blender, and enjoyed standing over the floor furnace in the winter to drink frozen daiquiris. Another great invention of the era was the attic fan. It was a large fan enclosed in a big box that was built above a trap door in the attic, usually in the hallway in the center of the house. Once the trap door was opened and the fan turned on, it pulled air into the house from outside.

In the early '50s, window unit air-conditioners became the first form of reasonably priced air-conditioning and stores began to spring up that sold only window units. Knox Street was literally lined with them. Some of those early companies were Avalon Appliance Co., Ed Kellum, and J. G. Boyd's Good Housekeeping Shop.

With the advent of reasonable prices for air-conditioning came a slump in new car sales. Many dealers were told that their competition was not other auto makes, but the fact that people were spending their money to buy window units to keep cool at home during the hot summer months rather than buying new cars.

9223 San Fernando – Newly constructed in 1948

In the early years after moving into our new home, we subscribed to the *White Rocker* newspaper. It was edited and produced by Hack Miller and his wife in their garage on Diceman, in the addition now known as "Little Forest Hills."

The only structures in what is now Casa Linda shopping center were Jim Smith's Mobil station, Casa Linda Theater, and a small convenience store known as the "Quickie." The streets were laid out, but there was no other construction.

That was soon to change. Right after the groundbreaking of Casa Linda Plaza, J.D. Crow built an adjacent center on the north side of Garland Road called Lake Park. I checked on the construction each day when I got off work. This was quite easy, as the house was only a few miles east from where we had been living.

One evening while on my way to the new home site, I saw a Whizzer motorbike parked in the front yard of a house on Garland Road. It had a price tag of $50 on it. As a kid, I always wanted a motorbike, and here was my opportunity to finally satisfy that desire.

We had a lot of fun with that Whizzer, and rode it from our duplex out to White Rock Lake on several occasions. It was just a short distance.

It came in handy once when Barbara had to ride it out to the lake to get me when someone was trying to reach me. We ultimately sold the bike for the same amount we paid for it. Incidentally, the Whizzer is being manufactured new again, but the selling price today is $1,700.

With all these new innovations life was changing, and part of the change was due to things like frozen foods, homogenized milk, boxed cake mixes, home permanents (Toni), and automatic washing machines and dryers.

Consumers were being introduced to all sorts of labor saving devices, and they took to them readily.

Ours was one of the first homes in the neighborhood to have a TV. It was a 10" Motorola, black and white of course, but a marvel nonetheless. In the beginning there was only one station, Channel 5 NBC, but others soon followed. Even our cat Blackie liked to watch "Kukla, Fran, and Ollie." Little did we know back then how much all of these modern new conveniences would change our lifestyles.

We were now into the early '50s and a building boom was in full swing. Many new additions to Dallas were being constructed on the fringes of the city.

Building materials were still in short supply and some builders would station a man on the highway approaching Dallas from East Texas. They would stop trucks loaded with lumber to find out if the load was already sold or might be available. A lot of it was green East Texas bull pine and not the best quality, but many of the low-priced homes going up in the projects were built from this material.

There were many items that remained in short supply since production was unable to meet the demand that had built up over the war years. Automobiles, refrigerators, home appliances, and furniture were all in great demand.

Cars were especially sought after, and some dealers were taking the more desirable models to California where the market was much stronger. The OPA still had ceiling prices on new and used cars, but it was not very effective since there were many ways around it, the most common being the under-pricing of a buyer's trade-in. If you didn't have a trade-in that the dealer could buy far below the market price, you quite often were unable to buy a new car. Many dealers would take cash under the table while invoicing the buyer at the OPA ceiling price.

Gas rationing was over, and Americans took to the roads like never before. We took our first trip to California in 1949 to visit relatives on both Barbara's and my side of the family.

We had a 1946 DeSoto that preceded air-conditioned automobiles, and if you have ever taken a trip across the Mojave Desert in the summertime you will understand our apprehension. To help us endure the expected intolerable heat, we borrowed an evaporative cooler that hung on the passenger window and began our journey. Needless to say, all it accomplished was to provide a sauna-like environment inside the car, as well as collecting numerous unwanted bugs that tended to die and sour in the water, causing a rather unpleasant aroma to fill the car. When we got home we immediately returned the cooler to its owner.

Chapter Twelve

The Fabulous '50s

Our family increased in 1952 with the birth of our son, William E. Mott III, and again in 1956 when our daughter, Catherine Elaine, arrived. Barbara was able to stay home and raise the children and we enjoyed our new home and family as many families were able to do on one income during the '50s.

During this time Dallas was in the midst of a terrible drought. The drought began about 1950, and we had no appreciable rain until 1957 when the dry period was broken by torrential rains.

The city scrambled for any and all alternatives to provide water to the citizens. One of the solutions was to pump water out of the Red River near Gainesville into a creek that fed into Lake Dallas. The water was extremely salty and resulted in a lot of rusted out water pipes and water heaters before their time.

They also dug a deep well down at the intersection of Buckner Boulevard and Northwest Highway. The water pumped from the ground at that location was so hot that they had to build a huge cooling tower in order to make it usable.

White Rock Lake was also reactivated as a water source, and people saved the wash water and bath water to use around their foundations and yards.

It was also illegal to wash cars with city water. Car wash companies had to use recirculated water, and the city built a ramp at the spillway of White Rock Lake to allow the do-it-yourselfers to drive their cars down on the deck below the spillway to take advantage of the trickle of water coming through the cracks in the spillway to wash their cars.

The Texaco station at Mockingbird and Air Line Road dug a deep well behind the station and was able to get a good water supply with which to wash cars.

A new dam had been built below Lake Dallas to create an even larger new reservoir that is now known as Lake Lewisville. It was predicted that it would take at least five years for the water to reach an acceptable level. Miraculously, the heavens opened up and in about seven days the lake was full and water was running over the spillway.

The water was so high that boats couldn't go under the bridge at I-35 in Lewisville. Once the new reservoir was filled, a portion of the old Lake Dallas dam was removed and the two lakes were allowed to merge.

I continued to be employed as a salesman for NAPA, or Motor Parts Depot as it was formerly called. We took a vacation trip with the children each year, alternating mostly between Florida and California.

Johnny Williams, the local Chris Craft dealer and a long-time friend, offered to pay our expenses on a trip to Florida if we would tow a boat and trailer down to his brother Jack in Fort Lauderdale. Jack had a small marina on one of the canals. When we arrived at Jack's house he was eager to launch the new boat for a trial run. We all got in the boat with Jack and the five of us set out to explore some of the numerous intracoastal canals in the city.

We pulled the boat up to a dock at the then-popular Pier 66, where a beautiful buffet lunch was being served. After eating we proceeded on out towards the ocean and were able to view Ft. Lauderdale from out in the Atlantic. It was quite an experience and our kids still recall it with great fondness.

After returning to Dallas, Billy began asking if there was any chance that we might get a boat. I talked to Johnny Williams, and we subsequently ordered a 22-foot Chris Craft four-sleeper cruiser.

We christened it *MOTT - YOTT V*, as we had had four runabouts

Taking the keys to Mott - Yott V – 1958

previously that carried the same name. We rented a boat slip at the Lakeview Marina on Lake Dallas for $50 a month, and met many new friends, as well as old acquaintances who had also moved their boats to Lake Dallas from White Rock.

Barbara enjoyed making curtains and decorating the cabin. While I was riding an aqua-plane behind speedboats on White Rock, skiing was a new sport in the late '50s, and Barbara and I learned to ski right away.

Bill III started trying to ski at the age of five, but at that time, there were no skis being made for children and he couldn't keep his feet in the bindings. By 1958, smaller skis began showing up on the market, and I bought a set for him. It was no time and he was up and skiing like a pro.

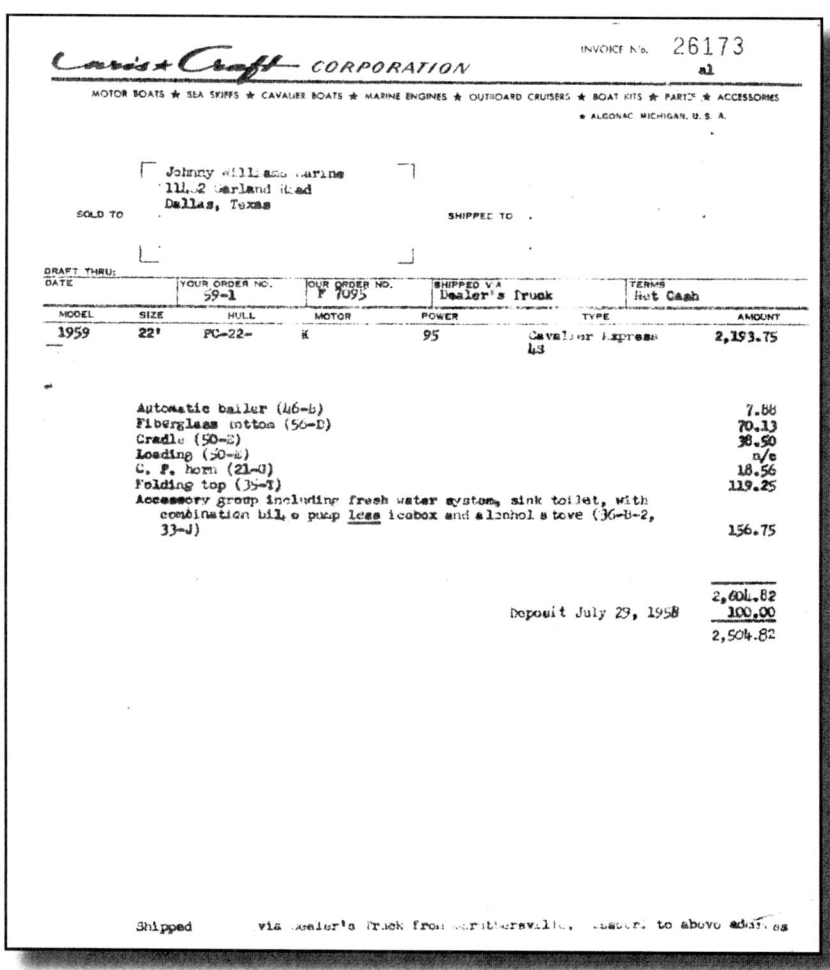

Invoice for Mott - Yott V – 1958

I had taken up the slalom ski about this time and was trying to coax little Bill to try it. He was still leery, however, and didn't really put out the effort to learn until Barbara learned how, and he couldn't stand his mom being able to do something he couldn't do. It didn't take him long to master it after that.

Barbara and friend Ruth Gipe at Lake Dallas in 1959

We hadn't owned this boat very long when Johnny informed us that Chris Craft was coming out with a new line of cruisers having much more powerful V-8 engines, and urged me to sell the 22-foot and order a new 25-foot. I sold the little 22 very easily, and we bought one of the new 1959 25-foot cruisers — *MOTT - YOTT VI.*

We continued to spend part of each weekend at the lake from 1958 through 1965. By this time, Bill III was beginning to show interest in old cars, and was asking if we could maybe find an old MG like he remembered Barbara and me driving when he was little.

We decided to sell the boat and begin searching for an MG to restore. We did, and enjoyed it until 1970 when we purchased a 27-foot Chris Craft up on Lake Texoma, and jumped back into boating until the oil crisis of 1972 began to cause gas prices to rise, at which time we sold it and closed the chapter on boating for good.

Chapter Thirteen

WHITE ROCK LAKE

Because of the continuing growth of the city, it became obvious a more reliable water source for Dallas was needed, and White Rock Lake proved to be a good alternative. The dam at White Rock Lake was begun in March of 1910 and completed in September 1911 at a cost of $800,000, thus creating a new reservoir for the city water supply.

Prior to the dam's construction, my father said he hunted rabbits and doves in what is now the bottom of White Rock Lake. Of course that area was way out in the country from the city and provided good hunting ground.

Before the dam was built, Swiss immigrants operated a dairy farm on land that became the basin of the lake. The Goforth family had a farm there that included the present-day Flag Pole Hill at the corner of East Northwest Highway and Buckner Blvd.

My friend David Goforth told me that the city just wanted to buy the bottomland, but that his father would not sell unless they agreed to buy Flag Pole Hill, which was of little use in farming. They had a very large farm that extended north and east of Flag Pole Hill and included much of what is now known as Lake Highlands.

Mr. Goforth drove a Model T Ford sedan, which his son David still owns, and one day while driving in downtown Mr. Goforth had a slight collision with a man driving a Cadillac.

The Cadillac driver was most irate and made the remark that it was just his luck to be hit by an old farmer in a Model T Ford. Little did he know that Mr. Goforth could have bought his Cadillac, several more just like it, and the dealership where it was purchased.

In 1923 a road was built all around the lake but it was not initially paved. My mother and father used to drive around the lake in their Model T Ford on Sunday afternoons like so many others did, and would be covered in white dust when they returned home.

Model Ts didn't have a gas gage but came with a stick that was marked to show how much gas was in the tank. My dad didn't have such a stick, and my mother said he would use a rolled up newspaper to find out how much gas was left. He did this so often that the newspaper finally deteriorated to the point that it began to disintegrate and clogged the fuel line.

The road was later named Lawther Drive in honor of Joe Lawther who headed the Park Department. During the Franklin Roosevelt Administration, sometime in the 1930s, a government program known as the Civilian Conservation Corps provided jobs for men to construct a rock retaining wall around most of the southern end of the lake. They also built the stone columns at the entrance off of Garland Road. An army type camp was constructed to house the young men who joined the CCC voluntarily. They planted many of the trees, built public restrooms and stone pavilions, and made a lot of the improvements that we enjoy around the lake today.

Initially, individuals and various companies could lease land around the lake for cottages as well as company-owned resorts. What is now called Tee-Pee Hill was the site of the Texas and Pacific Railroad's employees' clubhouse. It was a wooden structure with the interior done tastefully in dark woods, and thus it became known as T & P Hill. This building was torn down just prior to or in the early days of World War II when the Winfrey Point clubhouse was built.

Sol Dreyfus, who owned a men's fine clothing store as well as the Dallas baseball club, built the Dreyfus Club for his employees at another location around the shoreline near the bathing beach. The site was later acquired by the city and is still in use as Winfrey Point, which may be rented from the city for private parties. My Woodrow Wilson high school class had our 60th anniversary reunion at the Winfrey Point clubhouse in 2001.

A short distance from the lake entrance off Garland Road, there was a place to rent rowboats used primarily by fishermen. Down by the spillway was a little bait shop owned by a man named Buck Frank, where you could purchase minnows and worms, cold drinks, and fishing gear. This was in about 1928.

There were numerous private cottages built on the lake property around the shoreline, some of which were permanent residences and others were weekend retreats. In those days the water extended further north with the road around the lake utilizing an iron bridge off of what is now Goforth Road. Northwest Highway did not yet exist.

About 1929, during the administration of Mayor J. Waddie Tate, the spillway was breached and the water level was lowered to allow for the construction of a large concrete slab on the northeast edge of the lake.

This later became the White Rock Swimming Beach. The bathhouse, which still stands today, is the home of the White Rock Cultural Center. It was built at the same time and was constructed of poured concrete. The municipal concrete boathouses were constructed on the west side of the lake as part of the same project.

We still lived on Lindsley Avenue, and our neighbor across the street was a man by the name of Dick Mays. Dick operated the boat shop adjacent to the concrete boathouses, and was the dealer for Dodge Watercar speedboats. These were much like Chris Craft boats, but were built by the Horace Dodge Boat and Plane Company of Newport News, Virginia.

Horace was the son of one of the founders of the Dodge Motor Car Company. I presume Mr. Mays was required to buy several boats as part the Dodge franchise. He had a brand new 16-foot runabout in his garage, and his son Richard and I used to climb up and sit in the cockpit and dream about the day we might own one of these boats.

Mr. Mays also had a large hydroplane powered by a 12-cylinder, 550-horsepower Liberty aircraft engine. He ran it on White Rock Lake at speeds up to 60 miles per hour, which for that day and age was exceptionally fast on water. That year we experienced an unusually cold winter, and the lake froze over to the point that Mr. Mays was able to drive a Model T out onto the lake at about the place where the sailboats are today.

Subsequent to Mays' operation of the boat shop, a man by the name of Fred Slayter assumed the shop lease and was the first business on the lake to offer speedboat rides for 50 cents a person. Slayter operated two Dart runabouts of about 20 feet in length. These boats were in service for many years, and were later purchased by Johnny Williams, who continued to offer 50-cent boat rides well into the '50s.

As a young man I set several goals for myself: to marry a pretty girl, own a convertible, and have a mahogany speedboat on White Rock Lake.

I was two-thirds of the way there, so I started watching the newspaper for boat ads. I answered an ad for a 16-foot Dodge Watercar berthed in one of the concrete boathouses.

I finally had realized my childhood dream of one day owning a Dodge Watercar. We looked at the boat on a spring night in 1945 and agreed to buy it for $500 and assume the rental on the boathouse, which was only $50 a year. The boat had no neutral or reverse, but would run like the blazes forward! Of course I had to learn how to maneuver it without tearing down the dock.

Over the years, I've owned numerous speedboats and convertibles, but have always stayed with the same girl.

My long held goals and desires had been realized and I was only 22 years old. It amuses us now when we think back on our early priorities of having a boat before we had any furniture. Those were glorious days!

We were able to invite our friends and business associates to come out to the lake and have picnics and boat rides, which was a real treat since it was cool on the water and there was no air-conditioning in the homes.

In the summer evenings most of the people who owned boats would gravitate to the lake and we would enjoy each other's company with the men helping each other in working on their

Barbara and me in our 16' Dodge Watercar – 1944

respective boats, while the women would sit at one of the numerous picnic tables and visit.

Next to the concrete boathouses was a public pier that is still there to this day. Next to the pier was a two-stall pier under a roof, used by Johnny Williams to pick up and carry passengers. It was illuminated by strings of colored lights, which gave the entire area a festive appearance.

There was a refreshment stand in the immediate vicinity where you could buy hamburgers, soft drinks, ice cream bars, and candy. Weekends were teeming with people, both boaters and spectators.

When you were a boat owner there was no shortage of friends who would venture out to get a free boat ride. A cool ride up the lake to the vicinity of the swimming beach was very enjoyable, particularly in the evenings when the swimming beach was well lighted and filled with people frolicking in the water. It was a real jiving place.

Early in 1945 gasoline was still rationed and limited the amount of boat riding most boat owners could do. We were very fortunate since my friend Stuart Campbell was a Mobil gas dealer in Forney, Texas.

His major customers were farmers who had a virtually unlimited supply of gas coupons. He also accumulated some overage in warm weather after the gas in his tank truck expanded from the heat after being filled. He would bring a couple of five-gallon cans of gas out to the lake in exchange for boat rides.

Johnny Williams' docks – 50-cent boat rides and the Bonnie Barge *party boat – 194*
(Photo courtesy of Johnny Williams Jr.)

I'm sure that he felt this was a good trade, since gasoline was only about 15 cents a gallon and Johnny Williams charged 50 cents per person for a taxi ride in one of his boats.

I had gotten well acquainted with Johnny Williams in 1938 when he paid me to deliver circulars around the lake in my Model T Ford, advertising his boat rides to the picnickers.

After the war he would bring his engines to us at the shop for annual make-ready for the upcoming season. We would adjust the main bearings and grind the valves to make sure the engines would perform at peak efficiency.

Along about this time Chris Craft resumed production of boats. About the only thing that limited sales on White Rock Lake was the lack of enclosed storage facilities for the boats. Johnny delivered a number of 17-foot runabouts with 95 horsepower engines in them. While they performed quite respectably, they were no match for my little Dodge Watercar, which was now powered by a souped-up 100 hp. Mercury automobile engine. Johnny asked me not to challenge the new boat owners since he had told them that their new boats would be as fast as anything on the lake.

In addition to providing speedboat rides on the lake, Johnny came up with the idea that a large party barge would be a great attraction. He purchased two war-surplus steel barges that had been used to transport oil and gasoline on the Mississippi River during WW II. They were shipped to Dallas by rail and unloaded on a siding near the lake, and then trucked the remaining distance. They were quite large and were ultimately joined together side by side to form a big deck area.

In spite of the fact Johnny had only one leg as a result of a bad motorcycle accident during his youth, he worked diligently on this project and accomplished construction of a great deal of the superstructure of a lower and upper deck.

He also purchased a surplus propulsion unit known as a Sea Mule, which was attached to the rear of the barge.

It was a glorious thing!

She was equipped with a gasoline-powered generator that provided lights and music. It even had restrooms. You could hear it plying up and down the lake on a summer's evening with the colorful

Bonnie Barge *in all of her glory – 1945*
(Photo courtesy of Johnny Williams Jr.)

lights blazing and the jukebox blaring out "Across the Alley From the Alamo" by the Mills Brothers, along with other tunes of the day.

Johnny named the vessel after his wife, and it was known as the *Bonnie Barge*. It operated for several years until the city banned the operation of powerboats on the lake in 1950. Sometime after Johnny's operation was closed down and removed from the lake, his barge was transported by house movers to an open field, where it rested for several years.

He later sold it to the Drodz family who operated Lakeview Marina at Lake Dallas. There the main hull was put to work as a work platform for a dragline that was utilized to keep the shallows dredged out in the marina — a very ignominious end for such a stately old lady.

Johnny Williams Sr., giving rides to a group of orphans aboard his Bonnie Barge
(Photo courtesy of Johnny Williams Jr.)

One Saturday afternoon I was down at Johnny's boat ride concession near the swimming beach, and he was thoroughly exasperated with one of his taxi boats. It was a 19-foot Chris Craft runabout, which he had driven throughout the war years hauling passengers.

This particular boat had belonged to Curtis Sanford, who lived in one of the big houses next door to H. L. Hunt. The boat had developed a nasty habit of running very erratically in that when the ignition timing was adjusted so it would run properly at high speed, it would not idle. And when the timing was set so that the engine would idle, it would not develop sufficient power for high speed. Johnny was a man of very short patience and it had used up all he had. He was threatening to sink it, or burn it up, and he wanted to know if I would be interested in buying it.

I made a deal with him on the spot, giving him a cash deposit, with the agreement that I would be back on Monday afternoon with the balance to take delivery of the boat. Since new boats were available, I think he was anxious to take delivery of a new boat to replace this one.

After assuming ownership, I limped across the lake to my boat stall, No. 24, and began trying to determine what the trouble was. In the meantime, I put my Dodge Watercar on the market, and was able to sell it to a man who lived on Lakewood Blvd. near the lake, named Jim Tillery.

I had been able to obtain a second stall in the Municipal boathouses in which he could store his boat. I found the problem with the new boat to be very illusive, but before the week was over I discovered that a set screw designed to hold an idler gear had worn excessively, and the only repair required was to loosen the lock nut and adjust the set screw to hold the gear in place. After this was done, the engine ran beautifully and I couldn't wait to show Johnny how well it ran. He was greatly surprised and wanted to buy the boat back from me for $100 profit. I steadfastly refused after his insisting that was a good profit for two turns of a screw. But I had bigger plans for the boat, and Johnny never really got over it from then on.

To the west end of the boathouses was a shop with a marine railway. For a small fee a boat owner could rent the shop and pull his boat out of the water in order to do hull repairs. I had previously rented the shop when I refinished the hull and changed the engine in the Dodge Watercar.

We pulled the newly-acquired 19-footer into the shop where, with the invaluable direction and help of Ted Carter and Don Rhea, we refinished the hull, had the seats reupholstered, and recovered the floorboards with something akin to battleship linoleum.

Me at the helm of a 19' Chris Craft

When finished, the boat looked just like new and we enjoyed it for a couple of seasons. Later I found it impossible to turn down a very handsome profit and it went to a new owner by the name of Speck Frieden.

Speck was a nickname acquired mainly because of his freckles. His father had been a Dallas gambler who operated several policy wheels. He had been slain in gangland fashion, and rumor was that it was done on the orders of Benny Binyon.

Speck's mother was allowed to operate one policy wheel in Dallas that generated adequate income for her support and Speck's extravagant lifestyle. He later became a crop duster as well as a stock car and midget race car driver. He was a most colorful character and died at a very young age.

It was an early summer evening when I returned from my daily job, and I was preparing to settle down to a quite relaxing time at home. The telephone rang and it was Johnny Williams. He said one of his drivers had failed to show up and he wanted me to come down and fill in for him.

I agreed, and since it was only about five minutes from where we lived, I arrived in short order. The *Bonnie Barge* had already sailed with Mr. York as the captain. All at once the sky got dark, the wind began to blow, and a very vicious squall hit the lake. Johnny was quite alarmed in that he was afraid to bring the barge in with its tremendous weight and load of passengers since it could have easily destroyed the pier and boathouse if it came in at the wrong angle.

Johnny was on the dock frantically waving him away from the pier. As Captain York neared the shore he had the engine nearly wide open against the strong headwind, but without throttling back, he pulled the engine into neutral. The engine over-revved as a result and destroyed itself. This left him adrift with no steerage or power and the force of the gale drove the barge aground near the swimming beach.

In the meantime, Johnny's son, Johnny Jr., had just gotten out of a movie and arrived at the dock. In order to rescue the passengers and tow the barge back to the dock we climbed aboard a 20-foot Chris Craft runabout and headed for the barge.

When we got there, some of the passengers were scared to death, while others were still enjoying the party and the abundance of "refreshments" on board. We put a line on the barge and fastened it to the Chris Craft. We were unaware that there was a large amount of water in the bilge, and when we started towing the barge back to the dock the spinning drive shaft started throwing water up on the engine which was now in danger of being drowned out. I found a piece of a tarp and covered the ignition wires on the motor in order to keep it running.

We ultimately got the barge back to the dock and the party unloaded. The barge engine was so severely damaged that it had to be replaced. This took several weeks since it required getting an entire new engine. In the meantime, numerous parties had been scheduled for the barge and each evening it had to be towed away from the dock by one of the speed boats and anchored in mid-lake. This seemed to work very well since the generator unit was unaffected and the lights and music continued to function.

This was definitely a night to remember.

Chapter Fourteen

Racetracks, Race Cars, and Race Drivers

Back in the '20s and '30s, dirt track auto racing was a popular sport in Dallas. One of the early day tracks was located in the Trinity River bottoms near the Continental Street Bridge. After the building of the levees, this area became an industrial district with warehouses for Pittsburgh Plate Glass Company, International Harvester, and Ford Motor Company.

Jerry Cox, a longtime car dealer friend of mine, was an announcer for the races. There were several mechanics and machinists who built up race cars out of odds and ends of automotive parts.

My friends George and Warren Brown operated the Country Club Garage in Lakewood in the building that a Mexican restaurant has occupied for the past 50 years. Their race car was powered by an 8-cylinder Studebaker engine.

Another of the race car builders was Walter Allard, who operated a garage in Oak Cliff near the zoo. He was a pretty good machinist and designer and built a fast car.

Gene Frederick ran a shop on Main Street, which was a corrugated tin building with two large metal doors that they propped up each morning so that they would have some shade to work in. Gene built a beautiful little race car and had the axles and differential chrome plated. It carried a Roman numeral III. He raced his car at

Gene Fredrick dicing it up on the track in Oklahoma City
(Photo courtesy of Mitchell Rasansky)

the Love Field track, just across from the Hostess Bakery.

Most of the racing fraternity was made up of very close friends, and on certain nights of the week they would drive all the way to Houston to compete on a track down there, and on occasion, they would go to a track in Oklahoma City.

This was during depression times, and most of them couldn't afford a motel room, so they slept in their tow cars and drove back to Dallas the next day. One of the popular race car drivers at the time was Red Hodges, whose day job was driving a gravel truck.

I was afforded opportunity to drive one of these little midget racers through the kindness of one of my good friends, Hal Holsenbach. His car was fitted with the most desirable Offenhauser four-cylinder engine. The only way I can describe the feeling is to compare it to being shot from a slingshot. The acceleration was

breathtaking, and it cornered like it was on rails.
What a thrill!

Hal Holsenbach in his midget racer

There was a horse racing track at Fair Park belonging to R. B. George, the Caterpillar Tractor dealer. The track was sold to make room for the Texas Centennial in 1936, but the grandstands were retained.

After the Centennial, the land was converted to a dirt track for midget race cars, complete with the existing grandstands. Another horse race track was located right off Highway 80 in Arlington, Texas, known as Arlington Downs.

After pari-mutuel betting was outlawed in Texas, horse racing was terminated. The track was used for several meets featuring auto racing of the larger dirt track race cars, some of which had run in the Indianapolis 500. One of the popular drivers of the day at Indianapolis was Ted Horn, who showed up with his dirt track car in tow behind his '48 Lincoln Continental coupe. It added a lot of class to the occasion, and incidentally, he won the race.

Following WW II, several early-day stock car tracks were built around Dallas. One of the most successful was in an abandoned rock quarry in far East Dallas known as the Devil's Bowl. These races were primarily between pre-war Fords and Chevrolets, which had been modified to make them faster and suitable for racing.

This track was in operation for many years, and we could hear the noise from our home, which was a couple of miles away. On one occasion, my wife, Barbara, was chosen to reward the winner with a kiss. As housing development encroached, the track had to move from that location, and was later set up in Forney, Texas, where it is still in use.

These days, auto racing is held at the Texas Motor Speedway between Dallas and Fort Worth at a multi-million dollar facility with all of the fancy amenities that go with it, and it's a far cry from the crude accommodations of the early tracks.

Since I was gone all day long in the car covering my territory calling on customers, it was impossible for Barbara to go to the grocery store during the day or pursue any other errands she might need to take care of. I was still involved in buying and selling used cars, and while I usually had one on hand that she could use, there were many occasions when she had no transportation.

I had been smitten with English sports cars following their introduction to the American public following WW II. I discovered a 1947 MG TC stored in a warehouse on Hines Blvd. It was only three years old and had very few miles on it. The young man who owned it was being encouraged by his father, who never liked it, to sell it, and in return his father had agreed to buy him a new Ford.

The MG was in a much neglected state: it was covered with dust, the battery was dead, and the tires were low. It was jump started and driven home, and become Barbara's personal transportation.

This was a new experience for her since the MG was a right-

Barbara and her MG TC

hand drive, and had a four-on-the-floor transmission. She knew how to work a manual shift, but this was different since she had to shift with her left hand. She felt pretty special tooling around in such a sporty little car. In fact, the lady across the street, knowing our name was Mott, thought we were the owners of Mott's five and dime stores, and mistakenly assumed we were "well to do."

In 1947 S. H. Lynch had just started importing these English cars, MGs, Jaguars, and Rolls-Royces, and there were very few of them in Dallas at the time.

We joined a group of sports cars owners that gave us a social contact with many interesting people. We were having so much fun, we all decided to form a club, and agreed to call it F.A.S.C.A., which was an acronym for Foreign Auto and Sports Car Association.

We met weekly to talk cars and plan rallies and races. Some of the early members included the now famous car builder and former Le Mans race winner, Carroll Shelby, whom I had known since grade school, Mark Wilson the magician who later had his own television show in Dallas, Clarence and Eunice Talley, the current MG and Jaguar dealers, Jack Connolly, and Cully Culwell, the owner of the

Bill Mott

Varsity Shop across from SMU.

Carroll Shelby owned a chicken farm at the corner of what is now Central Expressway and Royal Lane, and drove a flatbed Ford truck.

Our friend and schoolmate Ed Wilkins, with Carroll's help, began building a hot rod of sorts. It had a tubular frame made out of galvanized water pipe and was powered by a flathead Ford V8. It was quite a sight, with no body, just the frame, motor, and wheels. Ed was so proud of it he drove it over to our house one cold winter night when there was actually snow on the ground.

Clarence Talley and his family were quite active in promoting the sale and activities of the cars. In fact, he used his influence with the county to have some roads blocked off at the corner of Church Road and Audelia Road, north of White Rock Lake, in what is now the Lake Highlands area, where we held an impromptu road race.

Of course, none of the participants had helmets, seat belts, or any of the other safety requirements taken for granted today. I was driving the MG and was in second place until I cut a corner too sharp and spun out on some loose gravel and nosed into an embankment.

My face hit the steering wheel and my lower lip was cut from mouth to chin.

One of the spectators drove me to Baylor Hospital where my lip was stitched back together. The little MG suffered a collapsed wheel, a bent frame horn, a broken transmission support, as well as slight fender damage. I repaired the car, but decided that racing was too expensive a hobby for me to pursue.

We went on to sponsor several sports car races at a nearby abandoned WW II airfield at Caddo Mills near Greenville, Texas, and laid out a 100-mile rally around Dallas County. It started at the Circle Grille on Harry Hines Boulevard, and ended up at the airport in Grand Prairie.

We also held drag races there that day. Participants came in all the way from Oklahoma, Houston, and other distant points where the interest in these cars had spread. It was at this meet that Carroll Shelby and Ed Wilkins brought the tubular framed hot rod, and Carroll recorded the fastest time of the day in it, and I recorded the fastest MG time.

Jack Connolly owned a camera shop at the corner of Lover's Lane and Inwood. It became a favorite hangout for Shelby, Culwell, and me to sit around and talk sports cars. Jack and his wife, Wilma, both had MGs, and within a short time, six more of our friends caught the bug and bought MGs too.

They were fascinating little cars, and we thoroughly enjoyed owning it until Barbara became pregnant with our first child, and the ride proved too rough to be comfortable.

We sold the car to our friend Ed Wilkins, and soon afterwards, Ed took the car to Norman, Oklahoma to a road race where he let Carroll Shelby drive it in his first road race, which he won. This proved to be the first of many racing victories for Shelby during his career as a driver.

Ed Wilkins in the MG I sold him, and that
Carroll Shelby won his first race in.

Chapter Fifteen

West End & Deep Ellum

Back during the "Roaring '20s." Dallas had become a flourishing warehouse and marketing center due to the arrival of the railroad. The northwest end of downtown became the place to be if you were looking to sell hardware, farming implements, furniture, crops, and the like.

As a result, many large brick warehouses were built to accommodate the expanding marketplace. As Dallas matured into the '60s and '70s, air transport became the new wave of efficiency with local businesses, and many of these grand old warehouses now stood empty.

Eric Jonsson, the current mayor at the time, began a push to convert the old warehouse district into a new entertainment and dining venue with the hopes it would attract new convention business to Dallas.

The Old Spaghetti Warehouse was among the first to open its doors in this new location, and it was built in a warehouse formerly occupied by a pillow and mattress factory. It was said that it took several weeks to get all of the leftover feathers cleaned up before they could start the rebuild.

It wasn't long before a familiar sight from the old days showed up in the form of horse-drawn carriages, in which you can still tour downtown Dallas today. It has been very successful, and now boasts nearly 100 restaurants and shops, and draws tourists from all over the world.

One of the more infamous attractions is the 6th Floor Museum, located in the old Dallas Schoolbook Depository building, which houses artifacts and information surrounding the assassination of President John F. Kennedy here in Dallas in 1963.

In the early Dallas years, Elm Street, to the east of downtown, was referred to by the black community living and doing business there as Deep Ellum. There was a theater, several jazz joints, bars, pawnshops, shoe shops, hubcap shops, and the like.

When I went to work for Republic Bank Dallas East in 1976, the area had been part of the Dallas scene for many, many years. Its location was east of Good Latimer Freeway, and extended several blocks to where the Texas and Pacific Railway crossed Main and Elm Streets. Several artists were living in the rear portion of some of the older warehouses and retail stores illegally because of the low rents. They were all wishing that the city would change the zoning to make it legal for people to live downtown.

Our bank decided to form a property owner's association so as to request a change of zoning from the City of Dallas. We met weekly in the boardroom of the bank, and invited city officials to participate.

This mushroomed into quite a ground swell of property owners, as well as prospective tenants hoping to locate in the area. The city was very agreeable to doing something with Deep Elm; however, they insisted that the property owners relinquish the ability to build high-rises as a consideration of the change in zoning.

This required getting the majority of property owners to agree to the changes. It took a considerable amount of time, due to a few owners who had aspirations of selling out to someone who wanted to build a skyscraper. They were very hard to convince, and some never agreed, but they were in the minority and we ultimately achieved the planned development.

It turned out very well, and many old buildings were turned into lofts and apartments, and made it possible for people to live and conduct business in the area. On Main Street, the city expanded the sidewalks, repaved the street, planted trees, and installed new street lights.

In keeping with old traditions, the name "Deep Ellum" was officially adopted for this revitalized new Dallas entertainment venue, and enjoys a vibrant nightlife today with abundant nightclubs, restaurants, and music theatres.

Chapter Sixteen

The '70s

By the '70s, Dallas was growing both commercially and culturally. Word was getting around that Dallas was where it was happening, and Republic Bank was referring to Dallas as "The City With No Limits" in their advertising campaign.

People began coming here for jobs, having heard that the economy was thriving in "Big D," and a lot of the country was still stagnant stage job-wise.

Large companies like Exxon, Mobil, Kimberly-Clark, H. Ross Perot's company EDS, Texas Instruments, which began in Dallas grew to a phenomenal size after the invention of the microchip, and the newly relocated American Airlines and JC Penney headquarters, became big factors in drawing people from other areas of the country to Dallas and Ft. Worth.

Following the surge of new businesses and industry, going into the '80s, the skyline over Dallas saw an ongoing change day by day as one building crane after another reared its spindly head over the town. In fact, the joke at the time was that the crane was the "official bird of Dallas."

The flying red horse on the Magnolia building had been the official emblem of the city for many years, but before long it was eclipsed by a mountain of new skyscrapers all around it. In years past, the main downtown business and social club was the University Club atop the Santa Fe Building, but each new skyscraper boasted of their fabulous new club on the top floor, providing a magnificent view of the unfolding metropolis. The civic leaders had the foresight and drive to make Dallas a distinguished city of culture as well as business.

LBJ Freeway was built around the north and east of the city to relieve the congestion on our inner-city roads and streets, and today, the new George Bush Tollway runs parallel outside of the LBJ loop to help relieve the congestion we now have on LBJ.

A new symphony hall was built, a museum of fine art was constructed in the same vicinity, and the Galleria shopping mall was located in the northern part of the city and featured a large ice skating rink and upscale shops.

Even the old Music Hall at Fair Park underwent a multi-million dollar face-lift. Later, the Nasher Sculpture Garden joined the arts district with its priceless collection of sculptures.

There are still big plans in the future to enlarge the arts district with an opera house and performance theaters. It was during the early '70s that Clint Murchison built the new Texas Stadium in Irving, and moved his Dallas Cowboys football team away from its original home in the Cotton Bowl.

If you wait long enough, history will come full circle again, and evidence of that comes with the Cowboys' recent announcement to move the team once again, this time to the bustling Arlington tourist center area in 2007.

EPILOG

The old Dickens quote of "It was the best of times, it was the worst of times" holds a lot of meaning to those of us that grew up during the "Great Depression" and World War II.

No one can look back and not have fond memories, even during the hardscrabble days. Human nature always seems to be able to make the best of any situation, and such was the case in the lives of my family and me. Enduring the struggles and challenges only made us stronger and more self-reliant, and people were tested in ways that brought out the best in them. Of course, then, like now, there were all kinds of folks, but for the most part, having to depend on oneself for survival made everyone appreciate the reward of knowing they had pulled themselves up by their own bootstraps.

There was no such thing as government aid, or food stamps, or organized charities. There were "Poor Farms" for the indigent aged, but no retirement homes with built-in assistance.

No, it was pretty much up to each person or family to handle their own problems. Neighborhoods were very close knit and helped each other when they could. We were all more or less in the same boat.

Life has been very good to me. I have had four vocations: sales, real estate, banking, and a busy retirement, and I have learned and grown with each new endeavor. My love of cars and boats has provided many pleasant hours in the company of good friends, some friendships going back many, many years.

These are exciting times in Dallas, and the future holds many challenges and opportunities. People today who were not around during the earlier years will make many memories like mine for their future families.

Each generation endures and enjoys the things that make life interesting, and each generation seems to be up to the task of meeting and making the best of whatever comes.

I hope they have as much fun as I had in my lifetime. I can truthfully say there is very little I would change if I had it all to do over, and I hope I have in some small way made a difference in the lives of those who have known me.

After all, that's what it's all about, isn't it?

Bill's Gallery of Boats and Cars

'39 Cadillac

Looking Back...

'47 Cadillac and '47 Chris Craft

Mom, Dad and Cathy and '38 MG TA

1958 T-bird

Bill's 19-foot Chris Craft on White Rock

Bill Jr. and Bill III in inboard dinghy

WILLIAM E. MOTT JR.

1922 – 2006

Bill was born and reared in Dallas, Texas during the height of the Great Depression, and was the epitome of what Tom Brokaw has tagged as the "Greatest Generation of Americans." He believed the old adage that "The harder you work, the luckier you get."

Bill was blessed with a true photographic memory and he created some of the most colorful and interesting memories a man can experience during a lifetime. From his days on White Rock Lake during the height of the wooden speedboat era before and after the war to the dawning of the great sports car movement in America in the late '40s and early '50s, he had a great love of old cars, boats, and any other vehicle of transportation, which is evidenced by the many stories he tells of his adventures of the era.

Starting out as a machinist in downtown Dallas, he honed his skills as a respected mechanic. He graduated into sales, and then moved into real estate, building his own real estate empire around North Texas. He eventually found his niche in banking and helped grow the fortunes of many other Dallas citizens while guiding and shaping some of the changes in the East Dallas area that are still prominent today.

The lofts in the Deep Ellum area east of downtown are now prized residential properties for the new executives working in the Downtown area because Bill had the vision back in the '70s and spearheaded a push for rezoning in the area that today allows artists and shopkeepers to live above their businesses and create residential rental property from old and long-forgotten warehouses.

He was present at the 1934 Chicago Century of Progress, and was at the gates on the opening day for the 1936 Texas Centennial that was responsible for the world's largest single collection of Art Deco architecture.

If you love Dallas like Bill did, you are in for a great stroll down memory lane during the "Good Old Days" from the Roaring Twenties to the New Millennium.

Willam E. Mott Jr., 2004